THIS BOOK
BELONGS TO

....

....

Thank you for Purchasing my book and taking the time to read it from front to back. I am always grateful when a reader chooses my work and I hope you enjoyed it!

With the vast selection available online, I am touched that you chose to be purchasing my work and take valuable time out of your life to read it. My hope is that you feel you made the right decision.

I very much would like to know what you thought of the book. Please take the time to write an honest and informative review on Amazon.com. Your experience and opinions will be of great benefit to me and those readers looking to make an informed choice.

With much thanks.

©COPYRIGHT 2024

The content contained within this book may not be reproduced, duplicated, or transmitted without direct written permission from the author or the publisher. Under no circumstances will any blame or legal responsibility be held against the publisher, or author, for any damages, reparation, or monetary loss due to the information contained within this book. Either directly or indirectly.

Legal Notice:
This book is copyright protected. This book is only for personal use. You cannot amend, distribute, sell, use, quote, or paraphrase any part, or the content within this book, without the consent of the author or publisher.

Disclaimer Notice:
Please note the information contained within this document is for educational and entertainment purposes only. All effort has been executed to present accurate, up-to-date, and reliable, complete information. No warranties of any kind are declared or implied. Readers acknowledge that the author is not engaging in the rendering of legal, financial, medical, or professional advice. The content within this book has been derived from various sources. Please consult a licensed professional before attempting any techniques outlined in this book. By reading this document, the reader agrees that under no circumstances is the author responsible for any losses, direct or indirect, which are incurred as a result of the use of the information contained within this document, including, but not limited to — errors, omissions, or inaccuracies.

Table of Contents

Introduction	5
Chapter 1: Whole30 Diet	8
Chapter 2: Instant Pot	19
Chapter 3: 100 Whole30 Instant Pot Recipes	26
Poultry Recipes	26
Seafood Recipes	60
Vegetarian Recipes	87
Soups, Stews and Broths Recipes	117
Meat Recipes	144
Side Dishes Recipes	160

Introduction

Are you really familiar with Whole 30 diet?
Do you know how convenient cooking by an Instant Pot pressure cooker?
Do you want to combine both Whole 30 Diet and Instant Pot cooking to have tasty and easy recipes?
Keep reading, this book will give you a perfect solution!

Just like there is a growing interest in healthy eating habits, there is a rising pressure from the hectic, and increasingly stressful world. The world is changing fast, and we constantly witness new lifestyles emerging, followed by new diets and new ways of cooking. **This book combines whole 30 diet with Instant pot cooking to serve you with a healthy and simple lifestyle!**

We know there is a direct and real connection between many so-called diseases of civilization (such as cancer, stroke, heart disease, autoimmune diseases, diabetes, and obesity) and modern diet based on grains, dairy and sugar.

The Whole30 diet was created to help you make a clean start.
After years of the so-called Western diet, which is unfortunately very tasty, cheap and convenient, your body is probably so full of toxins, your liver has to work overtime to process as much of it as possible. Detoxing requires a lot of energy, and instead of wasting it on detox, you should be using it for maintaining optimal health.

After 30 days of eating healthy, nourishing and cleansing foods, while abstaining from sugar, alcohol, and foods difficult to digest (ie grains and legumes), your body will feel light, your digestion will work smoothly, and you will suddenly have all this extra energy that will make you feel younger, stronger and more flexible. <u>By following a Whole 30 diet, you will get many benefits from it, below are some of them:</u>

- **Improved skin and hair condition**
- **Improved sleeping pattern**
- **You will feel more alert**
- **Improved energy levels**
- **Better digestion**
- **You become more clear-headed**
- **You lose weight**
- **Overall good health**

Instant Pot combines high heat and pressure to help you prepare fantastic meals with very little effort. It is a kind of electric pressure cooker, but it also has a number of features which enable you to cook food in different ways, eg pressure cooking, yogurt making, vegetable steaming, rice cooking, sautein, etc.

Instant Pot cooking style ensures the food you eat has preserved all the nutrients, color and aroma by being cooked quickly, and with a sealed lid that prevents liquid and nutrients escaping in the form of steam. Another reason Instant Pot has become so popular is that it saves time, and makes cooking even complex dishes, easy. Those who don't enjoy cooking, or who claim they can't cook, find Instant Pot is a true savior.

Learning how to use this gadget and experimenting with a different way of cooking is part of the fun. Besides, once you learn how to convert your favorite recipes into Instant Pot type recipes, you'll make your diet even healthier, while needing much less time and effort to make perfect meals.

Inside this book, we have provided 100 Whole 30 Diet recipes, which all are made by Instant Pot and well-chosen. You will find: **Meat, Poultry, Vegan & Vegetarian, Seafood, Soups, Stews and**

Broths, Side Dishes recipes. With so many easy-to-prepare but delicious recipes, your whole 30 diet will be full of fun and flavor!

To be healthy, you have to eat healthy, and as Bethenny Frankel so beautifully put it, "Your diet is a bank account. Good food choices are good investments". Welcome to the Whole 30 Diet Instant Pot cooking world!

Chapter 1: Whole30 Diet

What's so special about this diet?

Whole30 is not another fad diet, but a down-to-earth approach to healthy living. It focuses on foods that cleanse and nourish your body, and sets out a definite time frame of 30 days within which you can start experiencing the health benefits of the new dietary regimen.

The Whole30 diet revolves around the idea that if you change the way you eat, you will change the way you feel. In other words, when you remove unhealthy foods from your diet (although these are foods you probably eat most of), your whole body will experience a dramatic change. This change will initiate rejuvenation and indirectly, slow down the aging process.

Whole30 diet is very similar to the Paleo diet, in the sense that it allows meat, fish, fruit and vegetable, and bans processed foods, sugar, grains, dairy and legumes. However, the main difference between these two diets is their structure. While Paleo is meant to be a long-term eating habit and includes a lifestyle change (ie one should embrace the so-called Paleo lifestyle), the Whole30 requires a much stricter dietary regimen and is meant to be followed for only 30 days.

Whole30 diet revolves around <u>6 basic principles</u>:

➢ **It's based on whole, natural foods.**

Only foods which have not been processed are nutritious and truly healthy. Some of the most popular foods (chips, sodas, pizzas, processed meats and cheese, sweets, etc) are extremely unhealthy, although they are very tasty, thanks to the large quantities of flavor and color additives that go into them.

➢ **It's not meant to be a long-term diet.**

This diet is meant to be followed for only 30 days. The reason for a relatively short time you should be on this diet, is that it is quite restrictive. You are not supposed to eat any grains, dairy, legumes or sugars while you're on this regimen. This is required so that the body can self-cleanse from accumulated toxins.

> **It's very similar to Paleo, but follows a stricter dietary regimen.**

Whole30 diet follows most of the principles that apply to the Paleo diet, but is a stricter version of the Paleo diet. Paleo diet rules are more relaxed as this is meant as a long-term eating habit and lifestyle. For example, in Paleo you are allowed to occasionally have some alcohol or a cake made of almond or coconut flour, while in Whole30 no cakes are allowed, even if they are not made from grains. Paleo diet also allows natural sweeteners, such as honey, while the Whole30 bans all sugars, natural or artificial.

> **It's not too difficult to follow, provided you're used to eating healthy.**

When you read a detailed list of all the foods that are allowed on this diet, it doesn't look like a strict diet. However, this applies only to those who are used to eating healthy, ie who don't eat (or eat very limited quantities of) grains, sweets, dairy, and sugar. To them, living for 30 or more days without these foods may be a challenge for the first few days, but will not be a major problem.

On the other hand, if your typical diet is very unhealthy, ie if you eat a lot of fast food, sweets, cakes, sodas, processed meats, etc then you will struggle with cravings and may repeatedly slip. To solve this problem, you may consider adopting the Whole30 diet gradually, ie giving up grains for a week, but eating all the other forbidden foods. Then following week you give up grains and sugar, but eat all the other forbidden foods. Then the third week, you give up grains, sugar and legumes, and so on, until you can easily live on the prescribed Whole30 regimen for a month.

> **Meals should be freshly prepared and should consist of more vegetables than meat.**

As the Whole30 diet is based on natural foods, this means that packaged meals, the so-called TV dinners or take-aways should not be part of this diet. Ideally, food should be prepared prior to a meal, but the current pace of life doesn't always allow us enough time to cook fresh meals every day. So, plan your meals, and cook for couple of days ahead, so that when you come home after work hungry like a wolf, you don't grab the first thing that you find in the cupboard, while the healthy meal is being cooked. Although meat is allowed on this diet, it should be eaten in moderation, while vegetables (raw or cooked) should fill the bigger part of your plate.

> **You should have three meals a day.**

According to the Whole30 diet protocol, it's best to eat three solid meals a day. If you can't, or don't want to eat three meals a day, it's best to skip breakfast, rather than lunch or dinner. As for snacks, eat them only if you feel hungry between meals, although snacks are best avoided.

Benefits of Whole30 diet

What is possibly the most distinguishing feature of this diet is that it's not so much about how much weight you'll lose (which you will), or how much your health will improve (which it will), but to make you aware how certain foods affect your body, and why. The main aim of Whole30 is to encourage you to plan your meals strategically.

The best thing about this diet is that it can help you "reset" your metabolism, which in turn will revitalize your body through losing weight, improving your overall health and gaining muscle - and feeling great in the process.

Unless you cheat, you are bound to experience most of the Whole30 diet health benefits within a month. The most obvious ones are:

➢ **Improved skin and hair condition**

Your skin will glow, and your tone and texture will improve. This will be particularly evident if you have a problem skin or suffer from acne. The hair, too, will look healthier and fuller.

➢ **Improved sleeping pattern**

Once you start this diet you'll find that you fall asleep easily and you sleep throughout the night. This is important, because there are very few things that give you as much energy as a good night's sleep.

➢ **You will feel more alert**

You'll be surprised how "alive" you'll feel once you start this diet. Your concentration will improve and so will your performance at work or at school.

➢ **Improved energy levels**

After the initial adaptation period of a week or two, you will suddenly start having more energy than you've had in years, and the best part is, it will not fluctuate during the day.

➢ **Better digestion**

According to both Ayurveda and Traditional Chinese Medicine, it all starts in the gut. An increasing number of people are suffering from bloating, gas, constipation, stomach cramps, and other digestive disorders, usually caused by the unhealthy diet revolving around grains, dairy and sugar. Whole30 diet ensures clean eating for a month, which is more than enough for a body to self-cleanse itself.

➢ **You become more clear-headed**

Brain fog is becoming a common complaint among city dwellers. Feeling "foggy" usually means that there's a major imbalance in your body, usually brought on by an unhealthy lifestyle. The Whole30 diet, being the natural, nutritious and cleansing, can help you stay sharp and focused throughout the day, with no afternoon slump.

➢ **You lose weight**

Even if weight-loss is not your priority, once you give up sugar and grains, you'll start losing weight, whether you want to or not.

> **Overall good health**

When food becomes your medicine, you can maintain good health with minimal effort. It's not a difficult diet to follow, although you will have to give up some of your favorite foods, such as bread, pasta, alcohol, as well as sweets. Most people struggle for the first few days, but if you manage a week, you'll be fine. If for no other reason, then because by then you will already be enjoying some of the benefits of improved metabolism.

Foods you should, and shouldn't eat

The main idea behind this diet is to raise your awareness of how certain foods affect your body and mind. By first eliminating certain foods, and later (after 30 days) slowly reintroducing them into your diet, you'll become conscious of how your body reacts to certain foods.

Once you complete the Whole30 diet, it's best to introduce banned foods one at a time and pay attention to any adverse reactions, eg bloating, skin rash, stomach cramps, etc. That way you'll soon find out which foods to ban from your diet for ever.

Foods you should eat

> **Meat**

Only unprocessed meat is allowed (ie steak is OK, but salami isn't), and whenever possible buy organic or pasture-raised. Use in moderation.

> **Seafood**

Fish and shellfish are both allowed.

> **Vegetables**

You can eat vegetables, including potatoes, as much as you like.

> **Fruit**

Fruits should be eaten in moderation, because of their high sugar content.

- ➢ **Eggs**

Whenever possible, buy pasture-raised.

- ➢ **Nuts and seeds**

All nuts and seeds are allowed, except peanuts because they qualify as legumes.

- ➢ **Fats**

For the duration of this diet, you should only use olive oil, coconut oil and ghee (clarified butter).

Foods you shouldn't eat

- ➢ **Sugar**

This includes all natural and artificial sweeteners, such as sugar, honey, stevia, xylitol, etc.

- ➢ **Grains**

This includes all grains (eg wheat, rye, barley, oats, corn, rice, millet, bulgur, sorghum, sprouted grains), as well as the so-called pseudo-grains (eg quinoa, amaranth, and buckwheat).

- ➢ **Legumes**

This includes all beans, peas, chickpeas, lentils, and peanuts (including the peanut butter), as well as soy and all products of soy, eg soy sauce, miso, tofu, tempeh, etc. However, certain legumes are allowed, such as green beans, sugar snap peas and snow peas.

- ➢ **Dairy**

This refers to all kinds of milk (eg cow, goat or sheep) and milk products (eg cream, cheese, yogurt, sour cream, ice cream, etc).

- ➢ **Junk food**

Sweets, chips, snacks, cakes, processed meats, sodas, pizza, pasta, takeaways, etc.

- ➢ **Alcohol**

You should neither drink, nor use alcohol in cooking.

Create your own Whole30 diet plan

We are all different, and so are our nutritional requirements. To create a diet plan that will meet your personal requirements and preferences, you should take certain facts into account:

- **Your age**

You need fewer calories as you grow old, but that doesn't mean your diet should be less nutritious. On the contrary. As you reduce the amount of food, you should make sure that you still take all the necessary nutrients. On the other hand, young people who are developing mentally and physically, need food rich in calories, fats and carbs.

- **Your gender**

To support muscle development, men usually need more calories and protein than women. On the other hand, to preserve youthful complexion and delay skin aging, women should take more fresh fruit and vegetables, because of their high vitamin content, as well as high water content.

- **Profession**

This is also an important aspect of nutritional requirements. A miner requires much more calories and fats, than an admin clerk. On the other hand, students who are often under stress and who usually live a sedentary lifestyle, need to take lots of vitamins and minerals to help themselves stay focused, alert and healthy during this period of their life. For example, bananas are great for reducing stress, because they are high in potassium.

- **Environment**

Climate plays a very important role in a diet. Nutritional requirements in Norway or Australia are very different. While Norwegians will crave food rich in calories and fats, Australians will thrive on lean meats and vegetables.

- ➢ **Overall health**

Before you embark on any diet, make sure you have no health issues that could deteriorate further, and complicate your already compromised health.

- ➢ **Availability**

Some diets insist on certain foods which may not be available everywhere, eg plantain, tapioca, yam, etc. Besides, some diets require that you take specific supplements, which may not be available where you live, or could be too expensive to afford over long-term.

The key thing to creating your own Whole30 diet plan is to understand the Whole30 basics – what to avoid, and why. Creating an eating plan that takes into account your nutritional requirements and your personal circumstances, will help you get the most from any diet.

The biggest challenge of Whole30 is that foods that are banned are what we eat most of (eg bread, cereal, cakes, sweets, rice, pizza, pasta, sodas, processed meats, etc).

Tips for successful Whole30 diet

You'll most likely struggle the first few days, and may experience headache and cravings if you've been eating a lot of banned food until now, but:

- ➢ **Think of the benefits**

If you find this diet hard to follow, think about what you can gain if you stick it out for 30 days. Fortunately, most people start experiencing some of the benefits of this diet after about two weeks. You may even print out a list of all the benefits and stick it to your fridge, as a motivation not to slip.

- ➢ **Think it's short-term**

If you struggle giving up your favorite foods, just think how hard it would be if you had to give them up for the rest of your life. If you bear this in mind, 30 days will pass very quickly.

➢ Create a personal Whole30 menu

Study the basic Whole30 diet requirements, and recommended recipes, then draft a personal Whole30 menu. Whenever possible, buy fruits and vegetables that are organic, are locally produced and are in season.

➢ Plan a weekly menu

The best way to cope with this diet is to plan ahead. Make a weekly menu (for breakfast, lunch, dinner and snacks) and whenever possible cook ahead, so that when you come home after work you know there is an already prepared meal in case you're hungry and need to eat immediately. If you often get hungry between meals, make it a habit to always keep some healthy snacks in your bag, desk or a car, such as fruit, nuts or seeds.

➢ Shop accordingly

Vegetables are a major part of this diet, and as they should be bought fresh, if you know what you'll be eating during a week, it'll make your weekly shopping so much easier. You won't waste food or money buying items you know you are not going to cook that week.

➢ Networking

Ask a friend to join you on this diet, or find out about others who have experience with this diet through social networks. If you are new to dieting, you may need support, especially during the first couple of weeks. Sharing your experiences, recipes, or tips can make dieting not only easier, but fun.

The reason this diet lasts for only 30 days, is that that's how long it takes for everyone to start experiencing some, or all, of the benefits it brings. Of course, sticking to it for 60 days would be even better, provided you have coped well with the first 30 days. However, please note that this diet is not meant to be a long-term eating plan, and that after the initial 30 days, you can start reintroducing some of the "forbidden" foods, or you can go to Paleo diet, which is very similar, but less restrictive.

Following this diet may prove challenging if you often eat out, but with a little bit of forward planning while ordering a meal in a restaurant, you can avoid "slipping". However, if you occasionally slip, that's OK, that won't ruin your diet, but try not to. On the other hand, don't stress out if you do.

Frequently asked questions

> **Can vegetarians follow the Whole30 diet?**

There are different kinds of vegetarians. If you are a pescetarian (ie you don't eat meat, but eat fish) then you can follow this diet, because it allows seafood. If you are lacto-ovo vegetarian (ie you eat neither meat nor fish, but eat dairy and eggs), you can be this diet, although as you will not be eating meat, fish, diary or legumes, your only source of protein would be eggs. For 30 days you'll be OK.

> **Can pregnant women follow this diet?**

Pregnant women should not experiment with diets, especially restrictive ones, for their nutritional requirements are very high. They should always consult a doctor before deciding to change a diet.

> **Can I follow this diet if I'm on medication?**

If you are on heavy medication, you shouldn't. Talk to your medical practitioner.

> **What if I "slip"?**

Whole30 rules are very clear about this: if you slip, even if it's on day 29, you must repeat the whole process. However, many people do slip and do not repeat the diet from day one, and still experience many health benefits. So, it's up to you to follow this rule or not.

- ➢ **Can I stay on this diet for more than a month?**

If you are healthy and have not experienced any side effects, you can. Some people get so excited when they realize they are losing weight, or gaining muscle, or having better complexion while following a relatively easy diet, that they prolong the diet beyond the required 30 days.

- ➢ **What after this diet?**

The general advice is to gradually start reintroducing the banned foods into your diet, and monitor closely how your body reacts to it. If reintroduction of certain foods (alcohol, chocolate, processed foods, etc) brings back old problems (acne, bloating, insomnia, etc), at least you'll know which foods you should not be eating. However, once they complete the Whole30, most people switch to the Paleo diet. Paleo is a long-term diet, so it's much more flexible and therefore easier to stick to.

- ➢ **Can you stay on Whole30 diet indefinitely?**

Some people do, although in that case, your diet needs to be planned very carefully. A diet lacking essential nutrients can have very negative side effects, such as malnutrition, fatigue, or even chronic disease. It's best to discuss this with an experienced nutritionist.

Chapter 2: Instant Pot

Instant Pot combines high heat and pressure to help you prepare fantastic meals with very little effort. It is a kind of electric pressure cooker, but it also has a number of features which enable you to cook food in different ways, eg pressure cooking, yogurt making, vegetable steaming, rice cooking, sautein, etc. Take time to learn the basics, then start experimenting with all the different features this gadget offers.

Familiarize yourself with the new way of cooking

Whenever you buy a new gadget, be it a new car, laptop or a fridge, spend some time getting to know it. Although Instant Pot may be the most useful gadget you've ever had, to benefit most from its various features, you first need to figure out how it works.

Don't even think about using your Instant Pot before you've read the manual carefully, several times if you have to. Make sure you understand all the instructions, but the key to successful using this gadget is to start with simple meals, such as soups or stews.

Instant Pot can make cooking a pleasure. It has settings for cooking soups, stews, beans, rice, multigrain or porridge. Then, it gives you an option to cook, steam or saute. It has a timer, can cook food slow or fast, and will even keep it warm for hours, until you're ready to eat.

There are 14 models of Instant Pot. They vary in size, as well as in the number and kind of features they offer.

Specific features enable you to:
  1) **Cook different kinds of meals**
Options include: Soup/Broth, Meat/Stew, Egg, Porridge, Rice, Bean/Chili, Poultry, Congee, Multigrain, Cake, Yogurt.
  2) **Use different ways of cooking**

Saute/Sear, Steam, Pressure cooking, Slow cooking, Keep warm

3) Allows certain procedures

Pasteurization (eg of milk), sterilization (eg of baby bottles, or small pieces of equipment).

4) Extra features

- Altitude adjustment (eg eggs take different time to cook at the sea level, and on the 2000 meters altitude).
- One of the models (Instant Pot Smart) has the technology which allows you to program complex cooking methods on your smartphone/tablet and carry out the cooking wirelessly.

Dos and don'ts of Instant Pot cooking

You will find detailed instructions on how to use your particular brand of Instant Pot in your manual, these are just some general rules that apply to all types of Instant Pot.

7 basic rules to successful Instant Potting:

- Never add the ingredients into the Instant Pot, without putting in the Inner Pot first
- Never fill your Instant Pot to the max line
- Remember to use the Quick Pressure release knob, otherwise you may end up with the contents splattered around
- Don't forget to press the Timer button after you've filled and closed the pot
- Don't forget to turn the Venting knob into sealing position
- Follow the recipes instructions carefully, as you can't interfere with the cooking process once the lid is sealed (ie add more water or spice).
- Don't forget to put the Sealing Ring back in the lid before cooking begins

Useful tips for using Instant Pot

- You don't have to defrost food prior to cooking, it's best if you cook it frozen
- Instant Pot differs from the pressure cooker in that it operates on a slightly lower pressure. This means that cooking with Instant Pot takes a little bit more time, than cooking with the pressure cooker.
- The steel insert and the lid should be cleaned after each use. To prevent odors from previous meals affecting your current meal, try to clean the sealing ring as often as possible (ideally every time you use it). However, you should never clean the pot by immersing the base unit in water.
- Don't forget to add some liquid (water, wine, stock, etc) to the food that should be cooked in the Instant Pot. Always follow the recipe when it comes to the amount of spice or liquid, because you won't be able to add it additionally during cooking, for the pot is sealed.
- Don't attempt to make even simple dishes, such as soups, until you're clear how the Instant Pot works.

Advantages of Instant Pot

- Food can be cooked quickly. As Instant Pot is a kind of pressure cooker, most meals can be ready in about 20 minutes.
- Food can be cooked, sauteed, roasted or steamed.
- Cooking functions can be combined, eg you can first brown meat, then switch to pressure-cooking or slow-cooking.
- Food can stay warm for up to 10 hours.
- Although Instant Pot may look daunting, with lots of buttons and functions, the manual is user-friendly and explains everything in detail.

What you can and cannot cook in an Instant Pot

Dishes you can make in an Instant Pot:
- Cheesecake, brownies, rice pudding
- Risotto
- Beans, lentils, and rice dishes
- Dishes which require shallow pan-frying
- Cooked or fried eggs
- Curry
- Potato dishes
- Oatmeal
- Soups
- Stew
- Whole chicken

What you can't make in an Instant Pot:
- Bread
- Cookies
- Food that requires deep frying
- Meals that require stir frying
- Grilled meat

Where to buy and how to choose a good Instant Pot

Instant Pot is available through retail stores, so where you can buy it from depends on where you live. In the US, you can try Walmart, Kohl's, Sur la table, Williams Sonoma, Kroger, JCPenney, Target and if all that fails, you can always get it from the Amazon.

Instant Pots come in different sizes, models, and with different functions.

Size
Instant Pot usually comes as a 5,6,or 8 quart pot. 5 quart is suitable for 1-3 people, and 8 quart is suitable for large families, or when cooking for family gatherings, formal functions, etc.

Which one you'll buy will largely depend on how much cooking, and what kind of cooking, you intend to do with it.

Model
There are 3 main models

1. The Instant Pot Lux

This model has pressure cooking, slow cooking, steaming, rice cooking, sauteing and keeping warm features. It also has six different ways of cooking. If you've never used an Instant Pot before, this model is best to start with.

2. Instant Pot Duo

This model has all the features of the previous one, but it can also make yogurt.

3. Instant Pot Smart

This model has all the features of the previous two models, plus the digital interface on the pot itself. It also has temperature controlling, as well as cooking duration features.

Functions
Functions vary with the model, and price. Don't go for the most expensive and complicated one if this is your first Instant Pot. Rather, go for a simple model with basic features, until you are sure this is the kind of gadget you really need.

Besides, how much you'll use this kind of pot will depend on the diet you follow. If you eat mainly raw fruit and vegetable, then you are unlikely to use this pot often. On the other hand, if you enjoy cooked food, and especially if you have a big family, the Instant Pot may be the best investment you've ever made.

How to maintain an Instant Pot

To make sure your Instant Pot lasts more than one season, you need to take special care when cleaning it:
- Never apply force when cleaning the Instant Pot
- Never scrub it
- Soak it in hot soapy water and clean it gently with a sponge
- It's dishwasher safe
- To prevent burning, always use the Inner Pot
- Use non-stick cooking spray
- Follow the recipe instructions to prevent over-cooking

Approximate cooking time for different foods

Cooking time depends not only on the type of food you cook, but on the dish you are making, so these are only approximate times:

Meat
- Pork roast: 60 minutes
- Beef, ribs: 30 minutes
- Chicken, whole: 25 minutes
- Lamb, stew: 15 minutes
- Veal, chops: 8 minutes

Dried beans, lentils, grains, rice
- Soy: 30 minutes
- Dried beans: 25 minutes
- Lentils: 15 minutes
- Millet: 12 minutes
- Rice: 4-10 minutes

Seafood
- Fish, whole: 10 minutes
- Fish steak: 5 minutes

- Shrimp: 2-3 minutes

Vegetables
- Brussels sprouts: 4 minutes
- Broccoli: 3 minutes
- Carrots: 2 minutes
- Greens: 5 minutes
- Corn on the cob: 4 minutes

Fruits:
- Apple, peaches, pear, apricots (fresh): 2 minutes
- Dried fruits: 5 minutes

Chapter 3: 100 Whole30 Instant Pot Recipes

Poultry Recipes

Chicken Cabbage Curry

Serves: 4
Cook time: 30 minutes
Ingredients:

- 1 kg of boneless chicken, cut into small pieces
- 2 cans of coconut milk
- 3 tablespoons of curry paste
- 1 small onion, diced
- 1 medium red bell pepper
- 1 medium green bell pepper
- 1/2 head of a big cabbage

Directions:

1. Dissolve the curry paste into the coconut milk and stir well. Pour into the Instant Pot.
2. Add the chicken to the coconut curry mixture.
3. Chop both peppers into cubes and add to the pot.
4. Add the onion.
5. Cut the cabbage into slices and add to the pot. Make sure all the ingredients are coated with coconut milk.
6. Put the lid on, seal and cook on Low for 30 minutes.
7. When it's cooked, open carefully and serve immdietely.

Serving suggestion: Garnish with cilantro leaves or scallions.

Tip: Thai curry paste comes as Green, Red or Yellow. The green one is very hot, and yellow one very mild. For this curry I suggest the red curry paste, which is medium hot.

Chicken Salad

Serves: 6
Cook time: 20 minutes
Ingredients:

- 1 kg chicken breast
- 125 ml chicken broth
- 1 teaspoon salt
- ½ teaspoon black pepper

Directions:

1. Add all of the ingredients to the Instant Pot.
2. Secure the lid, close the pressure valve and cook for 20 minutes at High pressure.
3. Quick release pressure.
4. Shred the chicken. Store in an air-tight container with the liquid to help keep the meat moist.

Serving suggestion: Shredded chicken is great for sandwiches and salads, in which case you can add pickles, capers, olives, scallions, etc.
Tip: If you are cooking only 500 gr chicken, then reduce the cooking time to 15 minutes.

Lemony Chicken Casserole

Serves: 4
Cook time: 15 minutes
Ingredients:

- 2 tablespoons olive oil
- 200 ml chicken broth
- Juice of one lemon

- 1 kg chicken thighs
- 2-3 tablespoons Dijon mustard
- 2 tablespoons Mediterranean seasoning
- 800 gr red potatoes, quartered
- Salt and pepper to taste

Directions:
1) Add oil to Instant Pot.
2) Season the chicken thighs with salt and pepper and add to Instant Pot.
3) Combine chicken broth, lemon juice, and Dijon mustard, and pour over chicken.
4) Add quartered potatoes and seasoning
5) Place lid on Instant Pot and cook on Manual for 15 minutes.
6) Quick Release when the pot beeps.

Serving suggestion: Can be made in advance and used for picnic.

Tip: If you are not a fan of rich tastes, you can omit the mustard.

Chicken Tikka Masala

Serves: 4
Cook time: 10 minutes
Ingredients:
- 2 tablespoons olive oil
- 1 small onion, diced
- 3 cloves garlic, minced
- 1 (2-inch) piece fresh ginger, peeled and grated
- 1/2 cup chicken broth,
- 1 1/2 tablespoons garam masala
- 1 teaspoon paprika
- 1/2 teaspoon ground turmeric
- 1/2 teaspoon salt
- 1/4 teaspoon cayenne pepper
- 750 gr boneless, skinless chicken meat, cut into small pieces
- 450 g can tomatoes, juices included
- 1/2 cup coconut milk
- Fresh cilantro, chopped

Directions:

1. Set the cooker to the Sauté. Add the oil, and when it's hot, add the onion and sauté until softened, about 3 minutes. Add the garlic and ginger and cook until soft.
2. Add half of the chicken broth. Cook for couple of minutes, stirring all the time, add the garam masala, paprika, turmeric, salt, and cayenne pepper, and stir to combine.
3. Add the chicken and the remaining chicken broth and the tomatoes.
4. Close and lock the lid. Pressure-cook for 10 minutes at High pressure. When it's cooked, do a quick release of the pressure.
5. Stir the coconut milk into the sauce.

Serving suggestion: Serve on a bed of cauliflower "rice", or boiled potatoes.
Tip: Can be stored in the fridge for up to four days.

Juicy Whole Chicken

Serves: 6
Cook time: 30 minutes
Ingredients

- 2 tbsp olive oil
- 300 ml chicken broth
- 3 red potatoes
- 1 chicken, whole
- Spices of your choice, eg thyme, oregano, salt, garlic salt

Directions:

1. Put your Instant Pot on Saute, Low Setting.
2. Add olive oil and when it's hot, add chicken to the pot and lightly cook for about 2 minutes. Repeat with the other side. Turn off by pressing Cancel.
3. Remove browned meat from Instant Pot and add chicken broth, potatoes, and the chicken (whole or in pieces). Chicken should be on top of the potatoes.
4. Close lid, make sure steam valve is secure, and set to Poultry, normal setting, for 25 minutes. When it's cooked, do a quick release

Serving suggestion: Serve with roasted new potatoes.
Tip: Best served warm.

Spicy Lime Chicken Breasts

Serves: 6
Cook time: 15 minutes
Ingredients:

- 2 tablespoons zest lime

- 2 tablespoons honey
- 1 tablespoon lime juice
- 3 teaspoons mince garlic
- Salt and pepper to taste
- ½ teaspoon chili powder
- 1 ½ teaspoon paprika
- 1 teaspoon allspice, ground
- 1.5 kg chicken

Directions:
1) In a bowl, combine lime zest, honey, lime juice, garlic, pepper, sea salt, chili powder, paprika and allspice. Coat chicken in marinade.
2) Pour broth in Instant Pot, then add chicken.
3) Lock lid into place and seal steam nozzle.
4) Cook on High pressure for 15 minutes.
5) Naturally release pressure for 5 minutes then release any remaining pressure.
6) Open the Pot carefully, and serve.

Serving suggestion: Serve with roasted butternut.

Tip: Can be warm or cold.

Whole Roasted Chicken

Serves: 6
Cook time: 10
Ingredients:

- 1 whole chicken (about 2 kg)
- 1 tablespoon chopped fresh rosemary
- 1 1/2-2 tablespoons olive oil, plus a bit more for drizzling in pan
- 4-6 cloves garlic
- 1/2 teaspoon paprika
- Salt and pepper to taste
- Zest from 1 lemon
- 1 cup chicken broth
- 1 large onion, quartered

Directions:

1. Rinse the chicken with cold water and pat dry with paper towels. Place in baking pan and set aside.
2. Preheat Instant Pot and go to Saute mode.
3. In a small bowl combine rosemary, olive oil, garlic, paprika, salt, pepper, and lemon zest. After removing the zest, cut lemon in half and stuff in cavity of chicken. Spread spice mixture all over the chicken, spreading evenly. Drizzle some olive oil in your hot pan and place chicken breast-side down into pot. Leave for 3-4 minutes, until golden brown. Flip chicken over and bake the other side.
4. Remove chicken from pan and set onto the baking dish where it was before. Add broth to pan. Place onion on bottom of pan, place chicken on top (breast-side up) and secure lid.
5. Cook on High pressure for 6 minutes per pound. When it's cooked, wait for 10 minutes before releasing steam. Remove chicken and wait for at least 5 minutes before slicing.

Serving suggestion: Serve with garlic butter new potatoes.
Tip: Add 6 minutes cooking time per pound of chicken.

Italian Style Chicken Breast

Serves: 3
Cook time: 15 minutes
Ingredients:

- 1 tablespoon olive oil
- 3 boneless, skinless chicken breasts
- 1/4 teaspoon garlic powder and regular salt per breast
- dash black pepper
- 1/8 teaspoon dried oregano
- 1/8 teaspoon dried basil
- 250 ml water

Directions:

1. Set the Instant Pot to Saute, and add oil to the pot.
2. Season one side of the chicken breasts and once the oil is hot, carefully add the chicken breasts, seasoned side down, to the pot.
3. In the meantime, season the second side.
4. Cook about 3 to 4 minutes on each side, and remove from pot with the tongs.
5. Add 250 ml water to the pot, plus the trivet.
6. Place the chicken on the trivet.
7. Lock the lid, and cook on manual High for 5 minutes.
8. Allow the chicken to naturally release for a few minutes, and then quick release the rest.
9. Remove from the pot and wait for at least 5 minutes before slicing.

Serving suggestion: Serve with steamed broccoli.
Tip: Can be served warm or cold.

Rosemary Lemon Chicken

Serves: 4
Cook time: 14 minutes
Ingredients:
- 1 kg chicken breast halves
- 1 lemon, peeled and sliced into rounds
- 1/2 orange, peeled and sliced into rounds, or to taste
- 3 cloves roasted garlic, or to taste
- salt and ground black pepper to taste
- 1 1/2 tablespoons olive oil, or to taste
- 1 1/2 teaspoons agave syrup, or to taste (optional)
- 1/4 cup water
- 2 sprigs fresh rosemary, stemmed, or to taste

Directions:

1. Place chicken in the Instant Pot. Add lemon, orange, and garlic; season with salt and pepper. Drizzle olive oil and agave syrup (if using) on top. Add water and rosemary. Put the lid on the cooker and Lock in place.
2. Select the "Meat" and "Stew" settings for High pressure, and cook for 14 minutes. Allow pressure to release naturally, about 20 minutes.

Serving suggestion: Serve with cauliflower "rice".
Tip: You can use lime instead of lemon.

Easy Chicken Curry

Serves: 6
Cook time: 35 minutes
Ingredients:

- 3 tablespoons ghee
- 1 bay leaf
- 2 inch piece of cinnamon
- 1/2 teaspoon cumin seeds
- 4 medium-sized onions, chopped fine
- 1 tablespoon minced garlic
- 1 tablespoon minced ginger
- 2 tablespoon tomato paste
- 1 1/2 tablespoon coriander powder
- 3/4 teaspoon turmeric powder
- 3/4 teaspoon black pepper
- 3/4 teaspoon chili powder
- Salt to taste
- 1.5 kg chicken thighs or drumsticks
- 3 large potatoes, cut into cubes
- 1/2 cup chicken broth
- 1 1/2 tsp garam masala
- 2 tablespoons cashew paste(optional)
- 1/4 cup chopped cilantro

Directions:

1. In 'Saute' mode, melt ghee Add cinnamon, cumin seeds and bay leaf and stir till traslucent, being careful not to burn. Add onions, garlic and ginger, and saute till golden brown, about 7 minutes.
2. Add tomato paste mixed with 2 tablespoons water and stir.

3. Saute for about 3 minutes. If it sticks to the bottom, add some water.
4. Press 'Cancel' to turn off Instant Pot, otherwise spices can burn when you add them.
5. Add coriander, turmeric, black pepper, cayenne, salt and stir for a minute or two.
6. In 'Saute' mode, add chicken pieces and stir to coat with spice mixture.
7. Add 1/2 cup chicken broth and cook in 'Poultry' (or 'Manual' or 'Pressure Cook') mode for 15 minutes.
8. When it's done, do a Quick Release.
9. Add cubed potatoes and garam masala to chicken and stir gently.
10. Cook in 'Manual' or 'Pressure Cook' mode for 6 minutes. (Make sure steam release handle is in Sealing position)
11. Once done, do a Quick Release.
12. Add cashew paste (if using), stir the chicken curry and heat through in 'Saute' mode.

Serving suggestion: Serve with mashed potato.

Tip: Curry needs to be very spicy, but you can adjust seasoning to suit your taste. For a cashew paste you need to blend ground cashew nuts with water. You can use coconut cream instead.

Curried Chicken

Serves: 6
Cook time: 15 minutes

Ingredients:

- 2 tablespoons ghee
- 1 onion, chopped
- 2 tablespoons garlic, minced
- 2 tablespoons ginger, finely chopped
- 1 chili, sliced
- 2 tablespoons curry powder
- salt and black pepper to taste
- 1 kg boneless skinless chicken thighs, cut into small pieces
- 1 liter chicken broth
- 1 cup canned chopped tomatoes
- 3 cups fresh spinach, chopped
- 1 cup coconut milk
- 1/4 cup cilantro, chopped

Directions:

1. Melt ghee in 'Saute' mode. Add onions and saute until golden brown, about 2 minutes.
2. Add garlic, ginger, and chili and cook mixture until soft, about 1 minute.
3. Add curry powder, salt and pepper and cook, stirring for 1 minute.
4. Add chicken and stir to coat with spice mixture.
5. Stir in 1/4 cup of broth to de-glaze. Then, stir in remaining broth and tomatoes.
6. Close Instant Pot and cook on 'Manual' or 'Pressure Cook' mode for 5 minutes.
7. Allow the pressure to release naturally. Press Cancel and Open the Instant Pot.

8. Stir in spinach and coconut milk.
9. Cook soup in 'Saute' mode until spinach wilts and soup is heated through.
10. When cooked, stir in cilantro.

Serving suggestion: This curry has a soupy consistency and can be eaten as a soup, or a thin stew over cauliflower "rice".
Tip: Feel free to adjust the quantity of spice to suit your taste.

Creamy Coconut Chicken Curry

Serves: 6
Cook time: 10 minutes
Ingredients:

- 3 tablespoons green curry paste
- 450 ml can coconut milk
- 1 teaspoons coriander powder
- 1/2 teaspoon cumin powder
- 500 gr boneless chicken breasts or thighs, cut into small pieces
- 1/4 cup chicken broth
- 2 tablespoons fish sauce
- 1 tablespoon brown sugar
- 1 tablespoon lime juice
- 1 big green bell pepper, diced
- 2 zucchini, sliced
- 1 medium-sized onion, diced
- 1/2 cup sliced canned bamboo shoots
- 4 lime leaves, slightly bruised
- 1/4 cup Thai basil leaves

Directions:

1. Press 'Saute' and stir in rhe Green curry paste and 1/2 can of coconut milk until mixture is bubbly, about a minute or two.
2. Stir in coriander and cumin and cook for 30 seconds. Press 'Cancel'.
3. Stir in chicken, remaining coconut milk, and chicken broth. Close Instant Pot and make sure steam release handle is in the 'Sealing' position.
4. Cook on 'Manual' (or 'Pressure Cook') mode for 4 minutes.
5. Do a Quick Release of pressure and open the Instant Pot.

6. Add all the other ingredients - fish sauce, brown sugar, lime juice, bell pepper, zucchini, onions, bamboo shoots, and lime leaves.
7. Press 'Saute' and cook until vegetables are *al dente*, for 3 to 5 minutes.
8. Taste and adjust the seasoning and add the Thai basil leaves.

Serving suggestion: Serve with sweet potatoes.

Tip: Adjust the quantity of fish sauce, brown sugar and lime juice to suit your taste.

French Chicken Casserole

Serves: 6
Cook time: 18 minutes
Ingredients:

- 6 chicken thighs or drumsticks, bone-in, skinless
- Salt and pepper to taste
- 4 strips bacon, diced
- 1 big leeks, cleaned and diced
- 4 baby carrots, sliced
- 250 gr mushrooms, sliced or quartered
- 1 tablespoon tomato paste
- 1 tablespoon minced garlic
- 4 cups chicken broth
- 1 cup frozen pearl onions
- 4 sprigs fresh thyme (or 1 tsp dried thyme)
- 3 tablespoons ghee, softened
- 5 teaspoons flour

Directions:

1. Rinse the chicken and pat dry. Sprinkle both sides with salt and pepper.
2. Press 'Saute' and cook bacon until crisp. Press 'Cancel' and remove bacon; set aside.
3. Press 'Saute' and brown the chicken in batches. Remove and set aside.
4. Saute mushrooms and set aside.
5. Cook leeks and carrots till leeks are soft, about 1 minute.
6. Stir in tomato paste and garlic for about 1 to 2 minutes.
7. Turn off Instant Pot and use chicken broth to de-glaze.
8. Stir in chicken, broth, pearl onions and thyme and close the Instant Pot.
9. Cook on 'Manual' (or 'Pressure Cook') for 15 minutes.

10. While Chicken is cooking, mix together the softened ghee and flour.
11. Do a Quick Release of pressure and open the Instant Pot.
12. Stir in the sauteed mushrooms.
13. Press 'Saute' and drop the ghee and flour mixture into the Instant Pot, stirring until thickened.
14. Top each serving with bacon.

Serving suggestion: Serve with cauliflower mash.

Tip: You can leave the bacon out, although it will change the taste.

Spicy Chicken Drumsticks

Serves: 6
Cook time: 25 minutes
Ingredients:

- 1/2 cup ketchup
- 1/4 cup dark brown sugar
- 1/4 cup red wine vinegar
- 3 tablespoon soy sauce
- 1 tablespoon chicken seasoning
- Salt to taste
- 6 chicken drumsticks

Instructions

1. Combine ketchup, brown sugar, red wine vinegar, soy sauce, seasoning, and salt in the Instant Pot. Add chicken pieces and stir to coat.
2. Close Instant Pot Lid, and make sure steam release handle is in the 'Sealing' position.
3. Cook on 'Manual' (or 'Pressure Cook') for 12 minutes.
4. Do a quick release of pressure and carefully open the Instant Pot.
5. Remove chicken pieces and set aside.
6. Press 'Saute' and cook the sauce thickened, about 5 to 7 minutes.
7. Coat the chicken in the sauce and grill for about 2 minutes on each side.

Serving suggestion: Serve with salad and roasted potatoes.
Tip: You can make the sauce thicker, if planning to take this on a picnic.

Mediterranean Chicken Stew

Serves: 2
Cook time: 15 minutes
Ingredients:

- 2 tablespoons olive oil
- 1 medium-sized onion, chopped
- ½ of a small leeks
- 2 teaspoons mince garlic
- ⅔ cup celery sticks, chopped
- ⅔ cups carrot, chopped
- 750 ml chicken stock
- 1 red potato, diced
- 500 gr chicken breast, cooked and shredded
- 1 big eggplant, skinned and chopped
- 1 teaspoon thyme, dried
- pinch of paprika
- pinch of basil, dried
- pinch of oregano, dried
- 300 ml can chopped tomatoes
- 1 cup chopped kale

Directions:

1. Set the Instant Pot on Saute setting and heat the oil.
2. Add onions, leeks and garlic. Cook until translucent.
3. Add in celery and carrots and cook for 2 more minutes.
4. Add all the other ingredients: chicken stock, potatoes, chicken, eggplant, thyme, paprika, basil, oregano, diced tomatoes and kale. Cover and lock lid.
5. Cook on high pressure for 10 minutes.
6. Release pressure.

Serving suggestion: Serve with steamed vegetables on the side.

Tip: You can use cabbage as a substitute for kale, and zucchini instead of eggplant.

Creamy Mushroom Chicken Casserole

Serves: 4
Cook time: 25 minutes
Ingredients:

- 1 onion, sliced
- 2 tablespoons olive oil
- 1 teaspoon salt
- 800 g chicken thighs/breast, cut into small pieces
- 200 g mix of mushrooms (leave whole and halve the larger ones)
- 4 large cloves of garlic, diced roughly
- 1-2 bay leaves
- ¼ teaspoon nutmeg powder
- ½ teaspoon black pepper
- ½ cup chicken stock
- 1 teaspoon Dijon mustard
- ⅓ cup coconut cream
- 1 teaspoon arrowroot, corn or tapioca starch for thickening
- 2-3 tablespoons chopped parsley for garnish

Directions:

1. Turn the Instant Pot on and press the Sauté button.
2. Heat the oil, add onion and salt to the pot and cook for 3-4 minutes, until soft.
3. Add the chicken, mushrooms, garlic, bay leaves, nutmeg, pepper, stock cube, water and mustard and stir to coat. Then turn the Sauté off by pressing the Keep Warm/Cancel button.
4. Place and lock the lid, make sure the steam releasing handle is pointing to Sealing. Press Poultry (High Pressure, 15 minutes).
5. Once it's cooked, let the pressure release naturally for 5 minutes, then use the quick release to let off the remaining

the steam.
6. Open the lid carefully and press the Sauté function key again. Scoop a few tablespoons of the liquid into a bowl and dissolve in the arrowroot or other type of starch you have on hand. Return this mixture into the pot and stir through. This will thicken the sauce slightly.
7. Finally, add the coconut cream and stir through. Press Keep Warm/Cancel to stop the cooking process. Top with chopped parsley and serve.

Serving suggestion: Serve with roasted sweet potatoes.

Tip: You can use only one type of mushroom, or combine two or more.

Chicken in Vegetable Sauce

Serves: 6
Cook time: 1 hour
Ingredients:

- 1 teaspoon vegetable oil
- 6 chicken thighs
- 2 teaspoons salt
- 1 large onion, diced
- 1 stalk celery, diced
- 1/4 pound baby carrots, cut into 1/2 inch slices
- 2 tablespoons tomato paste
- 1/2 teaspoon dried thyme
- 1/2 teaspoon salt
- 3 cups chicken stock
- 450 gr can diced tomatoes
- 3/4 pound baby carrots
- 800 gr new potatoes

Directions:

1. Season the chicken with 2 teaspoons salt. Heat 1 teaspoon of vegetable oil in the pressure cooker and sear the chicken pieces for 4 minutes on each side, then remove to a bowl and sear the next batch. Once all the chicken is browned, pour off all but 1 tablespoon of the fat in the cooker.
2. Add the onion, celery, sliced carrots, tomato paste, and thyme to the pot. Sprinkle with 1/2 teaspoon salt. Sauté for 5 minutes, or until the onions are softened. Add a little bit of chicken broth to the pot, bring to a simmer, and scrape the bottom of the pot to loosen any browned bits. Simmer until reduced by half – about 3 minutes.

3. Stir in the remaining chicken broth, then add the chicken thighs and any chicken juices from the bowl. Pour the tomatoes on top, but don't stir. Put a steamer basket on top of everything in the pot – it doesn't matter that it's partially submerged – and put the potatoes and carrots in the steamer basket.
4. Lock the lid on the pressure cooker, and cook at High Pressure for 30 minutes. Let the pressure to come down naturally for 15 minutes, then quick release any pressure left in the pot.
5. Carefully lift the steamer basket of potatoes and carrots out of the pot, then scoop the chicken pieces out with a slotted spoon. Cut the potatoes in half, and then stir the carrots and potatoes back into the stew. Shred the chicken, and stir the meat back into the stew. Taste for seasoning.

Serving suggestion: Serve with roasted butternut.

Tip: Best eaten immediately.

Country Chicken Stew

Serves: 4-5
Cook time: 16 minutes
Ingredients:

- 2 tablespoons olive oil
- 1 big onion, chopped
- 2 medium-sized carrots, chopped
- 2 stalks celery, chopped
- 2 tablespoons minced garlic
- 450 gr can chopped red tomatoes (don't drain)
- 500 ml chicken broth
- 300 gr zucchini, chopped
- 1-1/2 tsp dried oregano
- ⅛ tsp cayenne (or more if desired)
- 3 medium potatoes, washed and cut to 1" chunks
- salt & pepper
- 6-8 bone-in chicken thighs, remove skin and trim fat
- 1-1/2 tablespoons balsamic vinegar
- 2 tablespoons fresh parsley, chopped

Directions:

1. Select Saute and allow the pot to get hot. Heat the oil.
2. Add onion, carrots, and celery and cook for about 5 minutes.
3. Add the minced garlic and cook for 1 minute
4. Add the tomatoes, zucchini, chicken broth, oregano, cayenne, and potatoes (see cooking alternatives for the potatoes above). Mix gently.
5. Season the chicken thighs with salt and pepper and add to the tomato mixture.
6. Select Soup and set the timer for 10 minutes (if you don't have a soup mode, choose manual, 10 minutes, High

pressure)
7. Use natural release for 10 minutes and then quick release.
8. Remove the meat and shred it. Discard the bones and return the shredded chicken to the pot.
9. Stir in vinegar and parsley.

Serving suggestion: Serve with grilled mushrooms and roasted sweet potato.

Tip: This can be refrigerated for up to 5 days.

Thai Red Curry with Chicken

Serves: 6
Cook time: 10 minutes
Ingredients:

- 3 tablespoons Thai Red Curry paste
- 450 ml can coconut milk
- 500 gr boneless chicken breasts or thighs, cut into small pieces
- 1/4 cup chicken broth
- 2 tablespoons fish sauce
- 2 teaspoons brown sugar
- 1 tablespoon lime juice
- 1 big red pepper, diced
- 2 medium-sized carrots, sliced
- 1 small onion, diced
- 1/2 cup sliced canned bamboo shoots
- 4 lime leaves, slightly bruised
- 12 Thai basil leaves

Directions:

1. Press 'Saute' and stir in red curry paste and 1/2 can of coconut milk until mixture is bubbly, about 1 or 2 minutes. Press 'Cancel'.
2. Stir in chicken, remaining coconut milk, and chicken broth.
3. Close Instant Pot and make sure steam release handle is in the 'Sealing' position.
4. Cook on 'Manual' (or 'Pressure Cook') mode for 4 minutes.
5. Do a Quick Release of pressure and open the Instant Pot.
6. Stir in fish sauce, brown sugar, lime juice, bell pepper, carrots, onions, bamboo shoots, and lime leaves. Press 'Saute' and cook until vegetables are *al dente,* 3 to 5 minutes.

7. Taste and adjust the seasoning, adding fish sauce, brown sugar or lime juice if necessary.
8. Stir in the Thai basil leaves.

Serving suggestion: Serve with roasted butter squash.
Tip: Adjust the amount of spice to suit your taste and use seasonal vegetables if these are not available.

Ginger Flavored Chicken

Serves: 6
Cook time: 15 minutes
Ingredients:

- 1 kg boneless, skinless chicken breasts (frozen OR thawed)
- 6 tablespoons soy sauce
- 3 tablespoons rice vinegar
- 1/2 tablespoon honey
- 3 tablespoons water, broth, or orange juice
- 2 tablespoons chopped fresh ginger
- 6 cloves garlic, minced
- 3 teaspoons corn starch

Directions:

1. Place chicken breasts in Instant Pot.
2. In a small mixing bowl, whisk together: vinegar, soy sauce, honey, water, ginger and garlic. Pour mixture over chicken and coat evenly.
3. Secure lid on Instant Pot and cook at High pressure for 15 minutes. When the meat is cooked, release steam.
4. Remove chicken breasts and place on a cutting board. Bring remaining sauce in pan up to a simmer (use the Saute feature on an electric cooker). Combine cornstarch with 3 teaspoons cold water and then pour mixture into pan. Simmer until sauce is thickened and the turn off heat.
5. Shred chicken and return to pot with sauce.

Serving suggestion: Serve with roasted potatoes.
Tip: Can be served warm or cold.

Chicken with Pineapple

Serves: 4
Cook time: 20 minutes
Ingredients:
- 8 oz can crushed pineapple
- Salt to taste
- 10 ml your favorite BBQ sauce
- 1 kg chicken breasts, frozen

Directions:

1. Add the crushed pineapple, salt, BBQ sauce and chicken to the Instant Pot. Cook frozen chicken on High pressure for 20 minutes. Turn the pressure valve to "Vent" to release all of the pressure.
2. Remove the chicken breasts from the pot and let cool. Shred the chicken.
3. Remove most of the liquid from the pot. Return the shredded chicken to pot and stir well.

Serving suggestion: Serve with roasted new potatoes.
Tip: Can be used for sandwiches or salads.

Buffalo Chicken

Serves: 6-8
Cook time:30 minutes
Ingredients:
- 2 celery stalks, diced
- 1 medium-sized onion, chopped
- 100 ml buffalo wing sauce
- 100 ml chicken broth
- 21 kg chicken breasts, frozen

Directions:
1) Add the celery, onions, wing sauce, chicken broth and chicken to the Instant Pot. Cook frozen chicken on high pressure for 20 minutes. Turn the pressure valve to "Vent" to release all of the pressure.
2) Remove the chicken breasts from the pot, and shred.
3) You can remove most of the liquid from the pot, or not.

Serving suggestion: Serve with roasted butternut.

Tip: Can be made ahead.

Seafood Recipes

Bass Filet with Shrimp

Serves: 4
Cook time: 11 minutes
Ingredients:
- 700 gr sea bass fillets, cut into chunks
- 3 tablespoons ghee
- 3 tablespoons Cajun, or Creole seasoning
- 2 onions, diced
- 2 bell peppers, diced
- 4 celery ribs, diced
- 600 gr tomato, diced
- ¼ cup tomato paste
- 3 bay leaves
- 1 ½ cups bone broth
- 500 gr medium to large raw shrimp, de-veined
- Salt and pepper to taste

Directions:
1) Season the fish fillets with salt and pepper. Sprinkle half of the Cajun seasoning onto the fish.
2) Put the ghee in the Instant Pot and press "Sauté". When the oil is hot, sauté fish for about 4 minutes, until it is evenly cooked on both sides. Using a slotted spoon, remove the fish from the pot and set aside.
3) Add the onions, pepper, celery and the rest of the Cajun seasoning to the pot and sauté for 2 minutes. Push "Keep Warm/Cancel". Add the cooked fish, diced tomatoes, tomato paste, bay leaves and bone broth to the pot and stir. Put the lid back on the pot and set it to "Sealing." Push "Manual" and set the time for just 5 minutes.

4) Once the fish is cooked, push the "Keep warm/Cancel" button. Carefully change the "Sealing" valve over to "Venting". Once the pressure has been released, remove the lid and change the setting to "Sauté" again. Add the shrimp and cook for about 3-4 minutes, or until the shrimp have become transluscent. Season with salt and pepper.

Serving suggestion: Serve warm or cold, on a bed of lettuce leaves.

Tip: You can also try other fish with this recipe.

Steamed Salmon

Serves: 2
Cook time: 3 minutes
Ingredients:
- 250 ml cold water
- 1/4 cup lemon juice
- cooking spray
- salt and black pepper to taste
- 2 frozen salmon fillets

Directions:

1. Pour cold water and lemon juice into your Instant Pot. Place a steamer rack inside; spray with cooking spray. Place frozen salmon fillets on the rack, skin-side down. Cover and close vent.
2. Set cooker to the Steam 2 setting; cook for 3 minutes. Release vent immediately when pot beeps. Season with salt and pepper.

Serving suggestion: Serve warm or cold, drizzled with melted ghee or a sauce of your choice.
Tip: Good for salads.

Clams in Garlic Butter

Serves: 4-6
Cook time: 10 minutes
Ingredients:

- 2 kg live clams
- 250 ml chicken stock
- 10 tablespoons melted ghee
- 2 teaspoons sea salt
- pinch seafood spice
- 500 gr baby potatoes, scliced in half
- Fresh lemon
- 1/2 cup parsley, chopped

Directions:

1. Wash the clams, discarding those that are opened.
2. Heat Instant Pot. Heat half the ghee and add potatoes. Saute for 2 minutes then add minced garlic and saute for another minute.
3. Pour in chicken stock and cook for about 3 minutes. Add salt and clams.
4. Lock the lid and close Pressure Valve. Cook on the Steam Setting for 1 minute. When Beep sounds, open the vent and wait for all pressure to release.
5. With a slotted spoon, remove clams and potatoes and transfer to a serving dish. Turn off Pressure Cooker and select the Saute function.
6. Simmer the liquid for 5 minutes and then add in the rest of the ghee and the parsley. Mix and then pour over clams.

Serving suggestion: Serve warm with a salad.
Tip: If using big potatoes instead of new potatoes, make sure they are cut into chunks.

Shrimp and Chicken a la Creole

Serves: 4
Cook time: 22 minutes
Ingredients:

- 400 gr skinless chicken breasts
- 500 gr raw shrimp
- 1 smoked sausage, sliced
- 1 big green peppers, chopped
- 2 celery stalks, chopped
- 1 big onion, chopped
- 300 gr frozen okra, chopped
- 1 tablespoon minced garlic
- 2 tablespoons chicken spice
- 450 gr chicken broth
- 2 tsp olive oil
- 4 tablespoons ghee
- 250 ml water
- 4 tablespoons flour
- 1 medium sized tomato, diced

Seasonings

- 1 bay leaf
- 1 teaspoon ground basil
- 1 teaspoon cayenne pepper
- 1 teaspoon oregano
- 1 tablespoon Creole Seasoning
- 1/2 teaspoon thyme
- 1 tablespoon Worcestershire sauce
- Salt and pepper to taste

Directions:

1. Turn the Instant Pot on the Saute function and add 1 tablespoon of the olive oil to the pot. When the oil is hot, add the sausage and cook for 2-3 minutes.
2. Remove the sausage from the pot. Add the ghee and remaining tablespoon of olive oil to the pot. While it melts add the flour gradually, whisking as you do.
3. Continue to whisk until the roux turns light brown. This should happen within couple of minutes. Press Keep Warm/Cancel on the Instant Pot so the roux does not burn.
4. Add the green peppers, celery, and onions. Stir and cook for 2-3 minutes until they are soft.
5. Add all of the seasonings, garlic, and Worcestershire sauce to the pot.
6. Add the chicken broth, tomatoes, and okra. Stir, and add the water.
7. Place the chicken breasts in the pot and return the sausage to the pot.
8. Close the pot and seal. Cook on Manual High-Pressure for 15 minutes. Allow the steam to release naturally for 10 minutes instead of quick release.
9. Remove the chicken from the pot and shred.
10. Place the Instant Pot on the Saute function. Add the raw shrimp and shredded chicken to the pot.
11. Cook for a few minutes until the shrimp turns bright pink.

Serving suggestion: Serve with a salad.
Tip: Very spicy.

Seafood in Tomato Sauce

Serves: 2
Cook time: 10 minutes

Ingredients:
- 1 tablespoon olive oil
- 1 medium-sized onion, chopped
- 2 garlic cloves, chopped
- 1 small carrot, chopped
- 1 quarter red pepper, chopped
- 130 g frozen mixed seafood, straight from freezer
- 600 ml fish stock
- 1 tablespoon tomato purée
- 1 teaspoon mixed herbs
- Salt and pepper to taste
- Fresh lime or lemon juice

Directions:
1. In the Instant Pot, press the Sauté button, add the olive oil and when it's hot, fry the vegetables for 3-5 minutes.
2. Add a little bit of water, and cook with lid off, for couple of minutes. Press Keep Warm/Cancel button.
3. Add seafood, stock, mixed herbs, tomato purée, a pinch of salt and pepper. Stir.
4. Press Manual button, and set to 5 minutes
5. When cooked, wait for a minute, then do a quick release. Remove the lid and let it rest for a couple of minutes. Don't worry if the sauce appears too thin, it will quickly thicken. Season with salt and black pepper and drizzle with lime juice before serving.

Serving suggestion: Serve with roasted new potatoes.
Tip: For more flavor, add some chili.

Shrimp, Chicken and Sausage Casserole

Serves: 10
Cook time: 35minutes

Ingredients:

- 250 gr shrimp, peeled and de-veined
- 1 tsp Cajun or Creole seasoning
- 1/2 cup + 2 tablespoons olive oil
- 500 gr skinless chicken thighs, cut into small pieces
- 250 gr smoked sausage, cut into slices
- 1/2 cup flour
- 1 big onion, diced
- 1 green bell peppers, diced
- 2 celery stalks, diced
- 1 tablespoon garlic, minced
- 1 liter chicken broth
- 450 gr can diced tomatoes
- 1 teaspoon white and black pepper each
- 1 teaspoon cayenne pepper
- 1 teaspoon dried thyme
- Salt to taste
- 1 teaspoon brown sugar
- 1 teaspoon Worcestershire sauce
- 2 teaspoon lemon juice
- 1 large bay leaf
- 300 gr frozen okra
- 2 tablespoons green onions (green parts only), sliced thinly
- Chopped parsley to garnish

Directions:

1. Rub shrimp with 1 teaspoon of Cajun or Creole seasoning and set aside.
2. Press 'Saute' and when Instant Pot has heated, add 2 tablespoons olive oil to inner pot of Instant Pot.
3. Add sausage and chicken, and cook until browned, about 8 to 10 minutes.
4. Press 'Cancel' and using a slotted spoon transfer chicken and sausage to a plate and set aside. To make the roux, press 'Saute' and add remaining olive oil and all purpose flour to inner pot.
5. Cook oil and flour until the mixture becomes light brown, stirring frequently so it doesn't burn. This will take about 10 minutes.
6. Add onions, bell pepper, celery, and garlic. Stir until vegetables are slightly soft, about 5 minutes.
7. Stir in broth, tomatoes, white, black and cayenne peppers, thyme, salt, brown sugar, Worcestershire sauce, lemon juice, bay leaves, and frozen okra.
8. Stir in reserved chicken and sausage.
9. Using a wooden spatula scrape the bottom of the inner pot to make sure there are no burnt bits stuck to the bottom.
10. Close Instant Pot and cook on 'Manual' or 'Pressure Cook' mode for 4 minutes. Do a quick release of pressure and open the Instant Pot.
11. Immediately stir in the shrimp and close the Instant Pot for 10 minutes. The shrimp will cook in the residual heat. Open the Instant Pot carefully and serve.

Serving suggestion: Sprinkle with parsley and green onions and serve with roasted new potatoes.

Tip: If you don't eat very spicy food, feel free to reduce the amount of spice.

Steamed Crab

Serves: 4-6
Cook time: 8 minutes

Ingredients:
- 1.5 kg frozen crab legs
- 250 ml water
- 1/2 tablespoon melted ghee for serving
- 1 tablespoon salt

Directions:
1) Place steamer basket into the Instant Pot with 1 cup of water and 1/2 tablespoon of salt.
2) Add the crab with 1 tablespoon of salt.
3) Secure the lid and make sure the valve is set to Sealing.
4) Press Manual and adjust the time to 4 minutes on High pressure.
5) When the Instant Pot beeps after 4 minutes, turn the setting to Venting, as this will allow quick release of pressure.
6) Wait for couple of minutes before opening the pot.
7) Transfer the cooked crab to a serving dish.

Serving suggestion: Serve with melted ghee.
Tip: This quantity of crabs has to be cooked in two batches.

Spicy Shrimp

Serves: 2

Cook time: 12 minutes
Ingredients:
- 2 tablespoons cornstarch
- 225 gr peeled large shrimp
- 1/4 cup low-sodium chicken broth
- 1/4 cup low-sodium soy sauce
- 2 tablespoons sugar
- 3 tablespoons rice vinegar
- 1 tablespoon chili paste with garlic
- 2 teaspoons dark sesame oil
- 1 cup broccoli florets
- 1/4 cup water
- 2 teaspoons olive oil
- 1/4 cup sliced green onions for garnish

Directions:
1) Combine 1 tablespoon cornstarch and shrimp in a medium bowl, set aside.
2) In a cup, combine remaining cornstarch, broth, soy sauce, sugar, rice vinegar and chili paste, and set aside.
3) Press Saute on the Instant Pot and add the sesame oil. When hot, add the broccoli florets and saute for 3 minutes.
4) Add water, then cover; cook for another 3 minutes until broccoli has steamed and water has evaporated.
5) Add the olive oil over the broccoli, followed by the shrimp. Stir fry and cook for 5 minutes, until shrimp is cooked through.
6) Add broth mixture to pan and toss the shrimp/broccoli mixture to coat. Cook 1 minute.

Serving suggestion: Serve with spaghetti squash and with hot chili sauce.
Tip: Best served warm.

Exotic Shrimp in Tomato Sauce

Serves: 4

Cook time: 5 minutes
Ingredients:
- 1 bell pepper, diced
- 1 medium onion, chopped
- 2 stalks celery, diced
- 2 cloves garlic, minced
- 2 teaspoons olive oil
- 1 tablespoon tomato paste
- 650 gr can crushed tomatoes
- Salt and pepper to taste
- 1/4 teaspoon cayenne pepper
- 1 teaspoon thyme
- 1 bay leaf
- 1 pound frozen jumbo shrimp (peeled and de-veined)

Directions:
1. Set the Instant Pot to Sauté and heat olive oil. Add the vegetables and sauté for 3 minutes, or until they start to soften. Add tomato paste, stirring, and cook for about another minute.
2. Add tomatoes, seasonings, and shrimp. Stir to combine. Cover with lid, making sure the valve is in the sealing position. Set the pot to manual High pressure for 1 minute. When finished, do a quick pressure release by moving the valve to venting. If the shrimp isn't fully cooked, set the pot to sauté and cook for about another minute, stirring constantly.

Serving suggestion: Serve sprinkled with chopped garlic.
Tip: Add chili for stronger flavor.

Shrimp scampi

Serves: 4
Cook time: 4 minutes
Ingredients:

- 1 kg shrimp
- 2 tablespoons olive oil or avocado oil
- 2 tablespoons ghee
- 1 tablespoon minced garlic
- 250 ml chicken stock
- 1 tablespoon fresh squeezed lemon juice
- Salt and pepper, to taste
- Parsley for garnish

Directions:

1. Place the oil or ghee in your Instant Pot, leaving the lid off, and set to Saute.
2. When the ghee has melted (1 minute), add the garlic and cook for 2 more minutes.
3. Add the chicken stock to de-glaze the pot.
4. Turn off the Saute setting, and add the shrimp and cover with the lid
5. Set to meat/stew mode and cook for 1 minute. Once cooked, allow for natural release for 5 minutes, then use quick release to release the remaining pressure. Season with salt and pepper.

Serving suggestion: Serve with fresh greens.
Tip: This quantity of shrimp may have to be cooked in batches, especially if your Instant Pot is small.

Lemon and Dill Fish Packets

Serves: 2
Cook time: 5 minutes
Ingredients:
- 2 cod fillets
- Salt, pepper, and garlic powder
- 2 sprigs fresh dill, or ½ teaspoon dried dill
- 4 slices lemon
- 2 tablespoons ghee

Directions:
1) Prepare 2 large squares of parchment paper.
2) Place a fillet in the center of each parchment square, and season with salt, pepper, and garlic powder.
3) On each fillet, place some dill, 1 or 2 slices of lemon, and 1 tablespoon of ghee.
4) Place a small metal rack or trivet at the bottom of your pressure cooker. Pour 250 ml of water into the cooker to to create a water bath.
5) Fold the parchment paper around fillet and seal, then place both packets on metal rack inside the cooker.
6) Lock the lid and set for 5 minutes on High.
7) Perform a quick release to release the cooker's pressure. Unwrap packets and transfer cooked fillets to a serving dish.

Serving suggestion: Serve warm, sprinkled with chopped parsley.
Tip: You can also try tilapia with this recipe.

Salmon with Avocado

Serves: 4
Cook time: 2 minutes
Ingredients:

- 500 gr salmon fillet, cut into 4 pieces
- Salt and pepper
- 3 tablespoons brown sugar
- 1 tablespoon chili powder
- 1 teaspoon ground cumin
- 1 teaspoon garlic powder
- 1 avocado, diced
- 500 gr cherry tomatoes, halved
- 1 teaspoon lime juice
- Chopped cilantro leaves, to garnish

Directions:

1) In a small bowl, combine the brown sugar, chili powder, ground cumin, and garlic powder. Spread over salmon with back of the spoon. Rub in.
2) Add 1 cup water to the Instant Pot insert and add steam rack. Place salmon onto the steam rack. Set to Sealing. Steam for 2 minutes. Wait for pressure to subside before opening the pot.

Serving suggestion: Serve with avocado tomato salad and roasted new potatoes.
Tip: Best served warm.

Easy Haddock

Serves: 2
Cook time: 20 minutes
Ingredients:

- 450 gr haddock fillets, fresh or thawed
- 350 gr can chopped tomatoes
- 2 tablespoons dried oregano
- 1 teaspoon black pepper and garlic powder, each
- ¼ cup fish stock
- 1 lemon

Directions:
1) Place haddock fillets at the bottom of the Instant Pot in a single layer if possible.
2) Mix tomatoes, oregano, pepper, garlic powder and fish stock in a small bowl and pour over fish.
3) Squeeze juice of half a lemon over the fish, and reserve the other half.
4) Cook on High for about 20 minutes. Remove carefully from the pot and transfer to a serving dish.
5) Slice lemon and serve on top of fish (optional).

Serving suggestion: Serve with roasted vegetables.
Tip: If cooking more fish, you need to increase the cooking time.

Pressure Cooker Salmon

Serves: 2
Cook time: 10 minutes
Ingredients:

- 2 thick salmon fillets, about 225 gr each
- ½ cup soy sauce
- ¼ cup water
- ¼ cup sherry
- 1 tablespoon sesame oil
- 2 teaspoons sesame seeds
- 1 clove garlic, minced
- 1 tablespoon freshly grated ginger
- 2 tablespoons brown sugar
- 2-3 green onions, minced, (reserve some for garnish)

Directions:

1. In a small bowl, combine soy sauce, water, sesame oil, sesame seeds, garlic, ginger, brown sugar, and green onions. Place salmon in two 6 inch square pans or two 8 inch mini loaf pans and pour half of the marinade over the salmon (reserve half of the marinade for serving). Allow salmon to marinate for 30 minutes in the fridge.
2. Add 1 cup of water to the pressure cooker pot and place trivet inside. Place the prepared pans inside. Secure the lid and turn pressure release knob to a sealed position. Cook at High pressure for 8 minutes.
3. While the salmon is cooking, pour reserved marinade into a small saute pan over medium high heat on the stove top. Mix 1 tablespoon of cornstarch with 1 tablespoon of water. Once the marinade comes to a simmer, slowly pour in the cornstarch mixture and whisk constantly until thickened, 1-2 minutes. Set aside.
4. When pressure cooking is complete, use a quick release.

5. Serve warm and drizzle the teriyaki sauce (optional). Garnish with reserved green onion.

Serving suggestion: Serve warm with roasted new potatoes.
Tip: For stronger flavor, add minced garlic to the potatoes.

Salmon and Veggies

Serves: 1
Cook time: 5 minutes
Ingredients:

- 1 frozen 225 gr salmon filet
- Chopped and sliced vegetables of your choice
- Your favorite seasoning
- Salt and pepper to taste

Directions:
1) Chop and slice your veggies and add them to a round cake pan. Season with salt and pepper. Cover the pan tightly with foil.
2) Add 1 cup of water to your pot, put the trivet in with the pan on top then lay a second trivet on it with the salmon on top.
3) Close and seal the lid.
4) Set pot to Manual 4-5 minutes.
5) Quick release the pressure when the pot beeps.

Serving suggestion: Serve with a vegetable salad.

Tip: By using different seasoning and vegetables, you will be creating a new dish each time you cook salmon.

Oyster Stew

Serves: 2
Cook time: 10 minutes
Ingredients:

- Two 450 gr cans of full cream coconut milk
- 1 cup bone broth
- 1 cup minced celery
- 500 gr jars shucked oysters with liqueur

- 2 tablespoons ghee or coconut oil
- 2 tablespoons minced shallot
- 2 cloves garlic minced
- ½ teaspoon sea salt
- ¼ teaspoon white pepper
- 2 tablespoon fresh parsley, chopped

Direction:

1. Melt ghee, saute shallot, garlic and celery until soft (about 4 minutes) Add the oysters, cream and broth
2. Close and lock lid, set to Low pressure and cook for 6 minutes.
3. Do a quick release. Stir in the sea salt and white pepper (to taste).
4. Snip the oysters using kitchen shears, if desired.

Serving suggestion: Garnish with parsley and serve in individual bowls.

Tip: You can add chili for stronger flavor.

Fish stock

Serves: 2
Cook time: 5 minutes
Ingredients:

- 4 white fish heads
- 2 carrots
- 1 celery
- 1 bay leaf
- Parsley with stems
- 6 Cups of water

Directions:

1. Add all the ingredients to Instant Pot
2. Set on High for 5 minutes
3. When cooked, release pressure

Serving suggestion: You can use as a soup, or as a stock to add to other dishes.
Tip: You can also use fish bones and tails to make the stock.

Wild Cod

Serves: 2-3
Cook time: 9 minutes
Ingredients:

- 1 large filet of wild Alaskan cod, frozen
- 250 gr of cherry tomatoes
- Salt, pepper and seasoning to taste
- 3 tablespoons ghee
- 25o ml water
- 3 tablespoons of olive oil

Directions:

1) In an oven safe glass dish that fits in your Instant Pot, place the tomatoes. Cut the larger fish fillet into 2-3 smaller pieces and lay on top of the tomatoes.
2) Season with salt, pepper and whatever other seasoning you are using.
3) Top each piece of fish with 1 tablespoon of ghee.
4) Drizzle with a bit of olive oil.
5) Pour 250 ml of water in the Instant Pot and place the trivet inside.
6) Set the oven safe glass dish inside and lock the lid.
7) Push Manual (High) and set the timer for 9 minutes.
8) Once cooked, release the pressure manually.

Serving suggestion: Serve sprinkled with chopped herbs and seasoning.

Tip: Can be used for salads.

Fish Soup with Cod

Serves: 6
Cook time:25
Ingredients:
- 2 tablespoon ghee
- 1 big onion, chopped
- 200 gr mushrooms, sliced
- 4 medium-sized potatoes, peeled & diced
- 1 liter chicken broth
- 1 kg cod, frozen
- 1 teaspoon fish seasoning
- Salt and pepper to taste
- 250 ml clam juice
- 100 gr flour
- 450 ml full cream coconut milk
- Optional: 4-6 slices of Bacon

Directions:

1. In your Instant Pot, place the trivet and add 250 ml of water.
2. Lay a few pieces of frozen cod on the trivet, lock the lid and close the valve, and cook on High (manual) for 9 minutes before releasing the pressure.
3. Remove the cod and put on a large plate, chop into large chunks.
4. In the meantime, dump the liquid out of the pot and remove the trivet.
5. Put the steel pot back in the device.
6. Press Saute, and add the onions, mushrooms, and butter, and saute until soft (2 minutes or so).
7. Add the potatoes, and chicken broth. Lock lid, and close the valve.
8. Push High (manual) for 8 minutes.

9. Once cooked, release pressure, and stir in fish seasoning, salt, pepper and fish.
10. Mix the flour with the clam juice until blended and pour into the soup.

Serving suggestion: Serve hot, sprinkled with coriander leaves (optional).
Tip: Can be kept in a fridge for four days.

Fish Fillets

Serves: 8 minutes
Cook time: 12 minutes
Ingredients:
- 4 white fish fillets
- 500g cherry tomatoes, halved
- 250 gr black Kalamata olives
- 2 tablespoons capers
- 1 bunch of fresh thyme
- Olive oil
- 1 clove of garlic, minced
- Salt and pepper to taste
- 300 ml water

Directions:
1) Put 300 ml of water into the Instant Pot, and add trivet or steamer basket.
2) Line the bottom of the heat-proof bowl with cherry tomato halves (to keep the fish filet from sticking), add thyme
3) Place the fish fillets over the cherry tomatoes, sprinkle with remaining tomatoes, crushed garlic, a dash of olive oil and a pinch of salt.
4) Insert the dish in the pressure cooker.
5) Set the pressure level to Low. Turn the heat up High and when the pan reaches pressure, lower the heat and let cook for 7-8 minutes at Low pressure. When it's cooked, release vapor through the valve.

Serving suggestion: Drizzle with olive oil and top with cherry tomatoes, olives, capers, fresh thyme, salt and pepper.
Tip: Can be served warm or cold.

Vegetarian Recipes

Potato curry

Serves: 4
Cook time: 25 minutes
Ingredients:

- 1 medium onion, chopped
- 4 large cloves of garlic, minced
- 1 kg potatoes, peeled and cut into chunks
- 2 tablespoons curry powder
- 500 ml water
- 200 gr carrots, sliced
- 200 gr mushrooms, sliced
- 400 ml can coconut milk
- 1 tablespoon sugar
- Salt & pepper to taste
- 1 teaspoon dried chili
- 3 tablespoons corn starch

Directions:

1. Set your Instant Pot to Saute. Cook the onions until translucent, then add the garlic and cook for one minute longer. Press the Keep Warm/Cancel button.
2. Add all other ingredients to the Instant Pot, except the cornstarch.
3. Set the Instant Pot to 20 minutes on Manual High pressure and allow the pressure to release naturally after this time.
4. Press Keep Warm/Cancel, remove the lid and press Saute. Put cornstarch into a small bowl or cup and mix into it a few tablespoons of water to make a thick paste. Pour it

into the Instant Pot stirring all the time. Add salt and pepper.
5. Taste and cook for about 5 minutes more until the gravy has thickened.
6. Serve immediately.

Serving suggestions: You can serve with cauliflower "rice".

Tip: Onions can be chopped or sliced. Sugar and chili can be left out. Amount of curry powder can be reduced if you don't like strong flavors.

Sweet Potato and Tomato Casserole

Serves: 4
Cook time: 11 minutes
Ingredients

- 1 large onion, finely chopped
- 4 tablespoons olive oil
- 2 teaspoons salt
- 3-4 large garlic cloves, crushed
- ½ red chili, sliced
- 2 tablespoons roughly chopped cilantro
- 2 teaspoons ground cumin
- 1 teaspoon ground coriander seeds
- 1 teaspoon paprika
- 550 g sweet potato, diced into cubes
- 400 gr chopped eggplant (no need to peel it)
- 2 cups chopped tomatoes
- 3 cups water
- 1 vegetable stock cube
- Juice of ½ lime

Directions

1. Press the Sauté key on the Instant Pot. Add the onion, olive oil and one teaspoon of salt and sauté for 5 minutes, stirring a few times.
2. Add the garlic, chili, cilantro, spices and the remaining salt and stir through. Add the sweet potatoes, eggplant, tomatoes, water and vegetable stock cube. Stir well and push Keep Warm/Cancel button to end the Sauté process.
3. Lock the lid. Press Manual, High pressure and set to 3 minutes. When the food is cooked, wait for 5 minutes and then push the quick release button to let the remaining steam escape.
4. Open the lid and stir in the juice of ½ lime.

Serving suggestion: You can decorate each serving with thinly sliced avocado, or roughly chopped cilantro.

Tip: Dishes that contain potatoes are best eaten immediately upon cooking.

Coconut Cabbage Curry

Serves: 4
Cook time: 11 minutes
Ingredients

- 1 tablespoon coconut oil
- 1 medium onion, sliced
- 1 + ½ teaspoons salt
- 2 large cloves of garlic, crushed
- ½ red chili, sliced
- 1 tablespoon yellow mustard seeds or powder
- 1 tablespoon mild curry powder
- 1 tablespoon turmeric powder
- 1 medium cabbage, shredded or sliced
- 1 medium carrot, sliced
- 2 tablespoons lime or lemon juice
- ½ cup desiccated unsweetened coconut
- 1 tablespoon olive oil
- ⅓ cup water

Directions:

1. Press the Sauté button on your Instant Pot. Add the coconut oil, onion and half of the salt and sauté for 3-4 minutes, until softened.
2. Add the garlic, chili and the rest of the spices and cook for 20-30 seconds.
3. Add the cabbage and carrots, lime juice, coconut and olive oil and stir through, then add the water. Press Keep Warm/Cancel button.
4. Place and lock the lid. Press Manual (High Pressure) and set to 5 minutes. Once the food is cooked, let the pressure release naturally for 5 minutes, then use the quick release to let off the rest of the steam.

Serving suggestion: Serve as a main dish with a salad, or as a side dish with chicken.

Tip: If you enjoy Oriental spices, you can add hot chilies or use medium or hot curry, instead of mild.

Garlic parsley mashed potato

Serves: 2
Cook time: 4 minutes
Ingredients:

- 4 medium potatoes, peeled, and cut into small pieces
- 1 cup vegetable stock
- 6 cloves garlic, peeled and cut in half
- 1/2 cup soy or other nondairy milk (or water)
- 1/2 cup minced flat-leaf parsley
- Salt
- Ghee, optional

Directions

1. Add the potato, stock and garlic to the Instant Pot.
2. Lock the lid. Bring to High pressure. Cook for 4 minutes. Quick release the pressure. Remove the lid carefully.
3. Mash the potatoes with a potato masher, a hand blender, or a fork. You can add all the milk (or water) or only some of it. Season with the parsley, salt, and ghee.
4. Serve hot.

Serving suggestions: When you dish the mashed potato on the plate, you can serve with a fried egg on top.
Tip: Instead of ghee, you can add one egg yolk to the mashed potato

Thai Red Curry with Mushrooms

Serves: 4-6
Cook time: 8 minutes
Ingredients

- 1 big onion, sliced
- 3 cloves garlic, crushed
- 1 teaspoon minced hot chili
- 2 kaffir lime leaves
- 1¾ cups vegetable stock
- 150 ml coconut milk
- 2 teaspoons Thai red curry paste
- 500 gr butternut, peeled and cubed
- 3 zucchini, sliced
- 200 gr oyster mushrooms, sliced
- 500 gr broccoli florets
- 1 to 2 tablespoons lime juice
- Chopped cilantro, for garnish

Directions:

1. Set Instant Pot to sauté. Add the onion and dry sauté for 1 minute. Add the garlic and chili and cook 1 minute longer.
2. Add the lime leaves, ¾ cup of the stock, the coconut milk, and curry paste. Lock the lid on the cooker. Bring to High pressure; cook for 3 minutes. Remove the lid once the pressure has come down naturally.
3. Add the zucchini, squash, mushrooms, and remaining 1 cup stock. Lock the lid back on the cooker. Bring to high pressure; cook for 3 minutes. Quick release the pressure. Remove the lid.
4. Stir in the broccoli. Lock the lid back on and let sit for 2 minutes. Carefully open the lid.
5. Transfer the contents to a large bowl. Add lime juice to taste, sprinkle with cilantro, and serve.

Serving suggestion: Serve with mashed potatoes.
Tip: Sliced kale can be used as substitute for broccoli.

Mexican Mushroom Sauce

Serves: 3
Cook time: 50 minutes
Ingredients

- 2 large mild chilies
- 1 teaspoon olive oil
- 1 bay leaf
- 1 large onion, thinly sliced
- 7 cloves of garlic, finely chopped
- 2 very hot chilies
- 1 teaspoon ground cumin
- 1/2 teaspoon dried oregano
- 1 tsp chili powder
- 1/4 teaspoon each, ground cinnamon and ground cloves
- Salt to taste
- 200 ml water or veggie broth
- 1 teaspoon apple cider vinegar
- 1 to 3 teaspoons lime juice
- Pinch of sugar, optional
- 200 gr sliced or chopped mushrooms of your choice

Directions:

1. Turn the Instant Pot on and press the Sauté button. Heat the oil. Add the bay leaf, onions, garlic and pinch of salt and sauté for 3-4 minutes, until softened.
2. Add the garlic, chili and spices and stir through for 20-30 seconds.
3. Transfer half of the onion mixture to a blender.
4. Add mushrooms to the remaining onion mixture in the skillet and a good pinch of salt and continue to cook over medium heat.

5. Add the hot chili to the blender. Add the rest of the ingredients, leaving out the vinegar and lime, and blend until smooth. Add this blended sauce to the skillet, (blend with 1/4 to 1/3 cup water). Cook for 5 minutes manual, then quick release after 10 minutes.
6. Cover and cook for 25 to 30 minutes until mushrooms are tender. Stir once or twice in between. Add more water if the sauce thickens too much. Add in the vinegar and lime and cook for another 3 to 5 minutes. Taste and dd more salt if necessary.
7. Remove bay leaf. Add a good dash of lime, freshly ground black pepper and salt and serve.

Serving suggestion: You can serve this sauce with mashed potatoes, or over roasted vegetables, or with spaghetti squash. Or, if thickened with a tomato paste, it can be used as a dip.

Tip: You can add 1 tablespoon tomato paste for a thicker sauce.

Spaghetti Squash

Serves: 2 – 4
Cook time: 6 minutes
Ingredients:

- 1 whole spaghetti squash (about 1200 gr)
- 250ml cold water

Directions:

1. **Cut the Spaghetti squash in half**
2. Scrape out the seeds with a spoon
3. **Add** 250ml of cold water and a trivet into the Instant Pot. Place the squash on the steamer rack, close the lid
4. Pressure cook at 6 minutes, then open the lid carefully.
5. Remove the squash from the pressure cooker. Remove the flesh by gently pulling it away from the skin with a fork to create long "spaghetti-like" strands.
6. Serve the squash immediately.

Serving suggestion: Serve the squash strands as you would spaghetti, with your favorite sauce.

Tip: Squash flesh needs to be pulled gently, otherwise it will break and may not resemble spaghetti at all. Should that happen, quickly mash the flesh and serve it as mashed squash instead.

Pumpkin Puree

Serves: 4
Cook time: 13 – 15 minutes
Ingredients:

- 1 kg pumpkin, halved with seeds scooped out
- 125 ml water

Directions:

1) Place 125 ml water in the bottom of the Instant Pot.
2) Place the pumpkin on the rack and cook at High pressure for 13 to 15 minutes.
3) Quick release and set aside to cool
4) Scoop the flesh out into a bowl and puree in blender, or with a potato masher, or with a fork.

Serving suggestion: Pumpkin has neutral taste and can be used in both sweet and savory dishes. If used for the main meal, it's best to serve it with melted ghee or olive oil. If used as a dessert, add cinnamon or nutmeg powder.

Tip: The more intense orange color of pumpkin, the richer in beta carotid it is.

Butternut Squash Coconut Curry

Serves: 4
Cook time: 10 minutes
Ingredients:
- 1 inch ginger
- 3 cloves garlic
- 1/2 onion, sliced
- 1 chili, diced
- 1 head cauliflower
- 1 butternut squash, seeded, peeled, and chopped
- 2-3 large carrots, sliced
- 3 sprigs cilantro, plus more for serving
- 450 ml coconut milk can
- 500 ml vegetable broth
- 1 tablespoon curry powder
- 1 teaspoon turmeric
- 1/4 teaspoon cumin
- 1/8 teaspoon fennel seeds
- 1/2 teaspoon black mustard seeds

Directions:

1. Add the vegetables to the Instant Pot.
2. Add cilantro, coconut milk, vegetable broth, and spices to the pot. Put the lid on, and press the Stew function at 10 minutes.
3. When cooking is done, release the pressure. Remove lid.
4. Garnish with cilantro sprigs.

Serving suggestion: Serve with mashed potatoes, cauliflower "rice" or boiled sweet potatoes.

Tip: This curry is best eaten mild, although if you prefer rich flavors, you can increase the amount of curry powder.

Mushrooms in Tomato Sauce

Serves: 4
Cook time: 11 minutes

Ingredients
- 1 medium-sized onion, thinly sliced
- 1 red bell pepper, very finely chopped
- 2 tablespoons vegetable broth
- 2-3 cloves garlic, crushed
- 100 gr button mushrooms, thinly sliced
- 200 gr tomato paste
- 100 ml vegetable broth
- 500 gr tomatoes, chopped
- 1/4 cup water
- 1 teaspoon brown sugar
- 1 teaspoon oregano
- 1 teaspoon basil
- 1 teaspoon red wine vinegar
- Salt and pepper to taste

Directions:

1. Saute onion and bell pepper on Low Saute mode until softened, 3 minutes. Add vegetable broth to prevent sticking.
2. Add garlic, drained mushrooms, and tomato paste. Stir until mixed thoroughly.
3. When sauce begins to stick to bottom, turn of heat and add some of the broth to de-glaze.
4. Add water, tomatoes, and spices and mix well.
5. Seal the lid, press Manual, High Pressure, at 8 minutes.
6. When finished, use Quick Release method to carefully release steam. Stir in salt and pepper to taste.
7. Transfer to a bowl. Serve hot.

Serving suggestion: Serve with cauliflower "rice".
Tip: You can substitute vegetable broth with water.

Simple Cabbage Dish

Serves: 2
Cook time: 10
Ingredients:
- 1 head of cabbage
- 1 small onion, sliced
- 2 teaspoons of garlic
- Salt and pepper to taste
- 300 ml of water

Directions:
1) Wash and clean the cabbage. Cut it into smaller pieces, to fit into your Instant Pot liner.
2) Place a trivet into the bottom of your Instant Pot Liner.
3) Add 250 ml of water to the bottom of your pot.
4) Place the cabbage in a dish that will fit on top of the trivet. Or, you may place the cabbage on top of the trivet directly inside your Instant Pot liner.
5) Add 50 ml of water, onion, garlic, and a dash of salt and pepper to the pot in pot along with your cabbage. If you are not using a pot in pot, you may skip the water in this step.
6) Close the Instant Pot lid and set to seal
7) Adjust temperature to Steam Mode for 10 minutes. If you do not have Steam Mode on your pressure cooker, you may set to Low Pressure for 5 minutes.
8) Once the cabbage is cooked, allow the pressure to naturally release for 10 minutes, then manually release any remaining pressure.
9) Carefully open the lid and take the cabbage out of the pot. Serve.

Serving suggestion: Serve with steamed vegetables, and roasted potatoes.

Tip: For a richer taste, you may add some soy sauce or spice to the cooking water.

Red Cabbage with Apple

Serves: 2
Cook time: 13 minutes

Ingredients:

Saute Ingredients

- 1 tablespoon olive oil (or broth to make oil-free)
- 1 medium-sized onion, finely diced
- 4 cloves garlic, crushed
- 550 g red cabbage, chopped
- 235 ml water
- 240 gr applesauce
- 1 tablespoon apple cider vinegar
- Salt and pepper to taste

Directions:
1) Use the Sauté setting over medium heat, and heat the oil.
2) Saute the onion until soft, about 3 minutes. Then add the garlic and sauté a minute more.
3) Add all the other ingredients and put the lid on and make sure that the vent is sealed.
4) Cook on Manual setting at High Pressure and set for 10 minutes.
5) Carefully move the pressure valve to release the pressure manually.
6) Serve immediately.

Serving suggestion: Serve with roasted pumpkin.
Tip: You can adjust the amount of applesauce and apple cider vinegar, based on whether you want the dish to taste sweet or sour.

Crispy Potatoes

Serves: 4
Cook time: 8 minutes

Ingredients:

- 500 gr Yukon Gold potatoes, peeled and cut into cubes
- 2 tablespoons of ghee
- Salt and pepper to taste
- ¼ cup Italian parsley
- Juice from ½ medium lemon
- 125 ml water

Directions:

1) Add 125 ml water to the Instant Pot, and add the potatoes.
2) Press the Manual or Pressure Cook button and program it cook for 5 minutes under High Pressure. Lock the lid, with the valve in the sealing position
3) When the potatoes are done, turn off the Instant Pot and let the pressure release naturally (about 10 minutes). The potatoes can be used right away or kept in a fridge and prepared in a few days.
4) Melt the ghee over medium high heat in a large skillet. Once the ghee is hot, carefully add the potatoes to the pan. Season generously with salt and pepper. Let them fry for one minute before browning the other side.
5) Season with the juice from half a lemon and toss with fresh chives or Italian parsley, adding salt and pepper to taste. Serve immediately.

Serving suggestion: Serve with a salad.

Tip: You can leave out both the lemon and parsley, and drizzle the potatoes with ketchup.

Boiled Potatoes

Serves: 4
Cook time: 10 minutes
Ingredients:

- 2 kg potatoes, peeled and chopped to medium size.
- Olive oil, or ghee
- 250 ml water

Directions:
1) Insert the steamer rack into the Instant Pot
2) Add about 250 ml water into the Pot and add potatoes
3) Close lid and turn the sealing vent to "Sealed"
4) Click the "Manual" button and reduce the time to 10 minutes
5) Once cooking completes let the pressure valve release naturally (about 20 minutes)
6) Open the lid and transfer the potatoes onto a serving dish.

Serving suggestions: Serve it immediately, as it's best eaten warm.

Tip: As a side dish eat it plain. As a meal of its own, pour olive oil, or stir in ghee into it and add salt and black pepper. To turn it into a salad, add sliced onion and some apple cider vinegar.

Simple Beets

Serving: 4
Cook time: 10 minutes
Ingredients

- 500 ml water
- 4 medium-sized beets, cleaned

Directions:

1. Add 500 ml water to the Instant Pot and place **trivet or steamer basked** into the Instant Pot.
2. Add beets, place lid and put on Sealing mode.
3. Turn Instant Pot on to high pressure for 10 minutes.
4. Once timer beeps, allow to sit another 14 minutes to steam. Carefully release pressure.
5. Remove beets from the Instant Pot, and allow to cool, before removing skins.
6. Slice thinly before serving.
7. Store in a sealed container in the fridge.

Serving suggestion: Serve with other steamed vegetables. To turn into a salad, add olive oil, salt and pepper, apple cider vinegar, and horseradish cream.

Tip: If you prefer *al dente* vegetables, reduce the cooking time to 7 minutes.

Mashed Potato Cakes

Serves: 3
Cook time: 10 minutes
Ingredients:

- 300 ml water
- 1 tablespoon ghee
- 80 ml milk
- 500 gr mashed potatoes
- 2 level teaspoons garam masala
- 1 teaspoon chili powder
- 1 teaspoon ground coriander
- 1 teaspoon ground cumin
- ½ teaspoon ground ginger
- ½ teaspoon salt
- 2 tablespoons corn starch
- 200 gr shredded cabbage
- 2 tablespoons finely chopped cilantro
- 1 tablespoon finely chopped chili
- ½ cup water
- 3 tablespoon olive oil
- 6 small sprigs cilantro, optional

Directions:

1) Heat water and ghee to boiling. Remove from heat; stir in the potatoes just until moistened. Let stand about 30 seconds or until liquid is absorbed (add a little bit more water if needed). Beat with fork until smooth. Transfer to medium bowl and let it cool.
2) Add the spices: garam masala, chili powder, coriander, cumin, ginger and salt, to the potato mixture, and stir to combine. Sprinkle cornstarch over mixture; stir to combine. Add shredded

cabbage, 1 tablespoon of the cilantro, and the chili. The mixture should be pretty dry.
3) In small bowl, mix remaining tablespoon cilantro with the water; stir to blend, and set aside.
4) Divide potato mixture into 12 equal-size balls, and flatten each one into a patty.
5) Heat oil over medium heat, and cook patties about 5 minutes each, turning once, until brown on each side and heated through. Transfer to paper towel-lined plate.
6) Garnish with cilantro sprigs.

Serving suggestions: Serve with salad.

Tip: Different types of potatoes soak up water differently, so to make sure you don't end up with a watery consistency, when adding water to mashed potatoes, use less than indicated in the recipe. You can easily add more, but if you add too much, you could ruin the mixture consistency.

Vegetarian Meatballs

Serving suggestion: 4
Cook time: 50 minutes

Ingredients

- 2 cups shredded kale
- 2 medium-sized carrots, cooked and chopped finely
- 3 tablespoons fresh thyme
- 5 tablespoons fresh parsley
- 1 cup walnuts, ground
- 2 tablespoons olive oil
- 1 small onion, finely diced
- 1 clove garlic, crushed
- salt and pepper to taste
- 1 egg
- 225 gr Portobella mushrooms, chopped into small pieces

Directions:

1) Use the Sauté setting on the Instant Pot and heat the oil over medium heat.
2) Saute the onion until it become transparent, about 2 minutes. Then add the garlic and sauté a minute more.
3) Add the mushrooms and cook for about 15 minutes, until almost all the liquid has evaporated.
4) In a medium mixing bowl, combine the kale, carrots, herbs, walnuts, mushrooms, egg, salt, and pepper. Refrigerate for at least one hour.
5) When ready, form into balls and bake for 30 minutes.
6) Alternatively, saute in Instant Pot.
7) Serve on spaghetti with marinara sauce and Parmesan cheese.

Serving suggestions: Serve with Spaghetti squash, or with the Tomato Sauce.

Tip: If you decide to saute the vegetarian balls in the Instant Pot, you'll need more oil than indicated in the recipe. They will be tastier cooked this way, although they will absorb a lot of oil.

Cauliflower Mushroom Risotto

Serves: 2
Cook time: 9 minutes

Ingredients

- 1 medium head of cauliflower, cut into florets
- 1 tablespoon ghee or coconut oil
- 1 small onion, diced
- 250 gr small mushrooms, sliced (shiitake, Cremini or white mushrooms)
- 3 garlic cloves, minced
- 1 cup full-fat coconut milk
- 1 cup vegetable broth
- 1/4 cup nutritional yeast
- Salt and pepper to taste
- 2 tablespoons tapioca starch
- Chopped parsley for garnish

Directions:

1. Grate or cruble the cauliflower into the size of rice.
2. Add ghee or coconut oil to the Instant Pot and set it to "Sauté."
3. When the oil is hot, add onion, mushrooms, and garlic and cook stirring for 7 minutes. Turn off the Instant Pot.
4. Add cauliflower rice, coconut milk, bone broth, nutritional yeast, and sea salt. Stir everything together.
5. Seal the lid, make sure the pressure valve is set to close, and set the Instant Pot to "Manual" for 2 minutes.
6. As soon as it beeps, immediately release the pressure valve and open the lid.
7. Sprinkle tapioca starch over the risotto and stir until thickened. Add more salt if desired. Add ground black pepper, if using.

Serving suggestion: Serve warm or cold, sprinkled with chopped parsley. Goes well with any salad.
Tip: You can substitute coconut milk with water, or white wine.

French Summer Casserole

Serves: 4
Cook time: 25 minutes
Ingredients:
- 350 gr medium-sized white mushrooms, washed and cut in half
- 100 gr Shiitake mushrooms, trimmed and cleaned
- 2 large red peppers, chopped
- 2 large yellow peppers, chopped
- 2 large green peppers, chopped
- 2 large zucchini, sliced
- 1 medium sized onion, finely chopped
- 2 garlic cloves, minced
- 1 tablespoon fresh coriander leaves, chopped
- Spices: ground ginger, cayenne, salt and pepper – ½ teaspoon each
- 2 teaspoons soy sauce
- Mediterranean herbs
- Olive oil

Directions:
1) Use the Sauté setting over medium heat, and heat the oil.
2) Saute the onion for 3 minutes or until soft. Add the garlic and sauté a minute more.
3) Add the peppers, mushrooms and zucchini, and continue to saute for 5 minutes.
4) Add all other ingredients to the Instant Pot and put the lid on, making sure that the vent is sealed. Cook on Manual setting at High pressure and set for 10 minutes.
5) Carefully move the pressure valve to release the pressure manually.
6) Season to taste, and saute for a further 5 minutes.
7) Serve warm, garnished with chopped fresh herbs.

Serving suggestions: Serve on a bed of cauliflower "rice".

Tip: Instead of Mediterranean herbs you can use fresh cilantro, basil or parsley.

Soups, Stews and Broths Recipes

Creamy Butternut Soup

Serves: 4
Cook time: 39 minutes
Ingredients

- 1 teaspoon olive oil
- 1 large onion, chopped
- 2 cloves garlic, minced
- 1 tablespoon curry powder
- 1.5 kg butternut squash, peeled, cleaned, and cut into small pieces
- 1 1/2 teaspoons salt
- 750 ml water
- 125 ml coconut milk or cream

Directions:

1. Press "Sauté" button on the Instant Pot. Heat the olive oil, add onion, and sauté until soft, about 8 minutes. Add in the garlic and curry powder and continue to sauté for 1 minute.
2. Turn the Instant Pot off for a moment, then add the butternut squash, salt, and water into the pot. Cover with the lid and seal the top. Select the "Soup" setting, and let the soup cook at High pressure for 30 minutes.
3. When the soup is cooked, wait for 10 minutes before releasing the pressure, or use the "Quick Release" method by turning the valve on the lid from sealing to venting.
4. Let the butternut cool slightly, then transfer it to a blender or food processor to blend until smooth.
5. Return the blended soup to the pot and stir in the coconut milk. Add the seasoning, taste and add some more, if

necessary. Garnish with parsley.

Serving suggestion: Serve warm.
Tip: Can be kept in a fridge for up to a week.

Potato Soup

Serves: 4
Cook time: 10 minutes

Ingredients:

- 500 gr dice Yukon Gold Potato
- 1 medium sized onion
- 4 garlic cloves, minced
- 1 teaspoon salt
- 800 ml chicken stock
- 100 gr bacon for garnish, diced and fried (optional)

Directions:
1) Add potatoes, onion, garlic, seasoning and chicken stock to Instant Pot.
2) Lock cover into place and seal steam nozzle.
3) Cook on High pressure for 10 minutes. Quick release pressure.
4) Hit cancel and then saute.

Serving suggestion: Serve with crispy bacon or chopped fresh parsley.

Tip: You can use non-dairy cream for garnish instead of bacon.

Quick French Onion Soup

Serves: 4
Cook time: 25 minutes

Ingredients:

- 2 tablespoons avocado oil, coconut oil, or olive oil
- 1 kg yellow onions

- 1 tablespoon balsamic vinegar
- 1.4 liter pork stock
- 1 teaspoon salt
- 2 bay leaves
- 2 sprigs of fresh thyme, or 1 teaspoon dried thyme

Directions:

1. Peel and slice the onions very thinly. Set the Instant Pot to "Saute" and add the oil. Once the oil is hot, add the onions. Cook the onions until soft, stirring frequently to prevent sticking, about 15 minutes.
2. Add the balsamic vinegar, then add the stock, salt, bay leaves and thyme. Turn off the Instant Pot and close the lid. Set the lid to Sealing position.
3. Set the Instant Pot to "High Pressure" and cook the soup for 10 minutes once it has come up to pressure. Allow the pressure to release using the "natural release" – about 10 minutes.
4. Discard the bay leaves and thyme stems, then blend the soup together either using an immersion blender directly in the pot, or by transferring the soup carefully to a blender.

Serving suggestion: Serve hot.

Tip: For a more rustic soup, skip blending.

Chicken Thighs Soup

Serves: 4
Cook time: 20 minutes

Ingredients:

- 5 large chicken thighs
- 2 large ribs celery, sliced
- 2 medium carrots, peeled and diced
- 1 large parsnip, peeled and diced
- 1 small onion, diced
- 2 bay leaves
- ½ teaspoon black pepper
- 1 liter chicken broth

Directions:

1. Layer all of the ingredients in the pot. Pour the chicken broth over the ingredients.
2. Cover the pot and set to "Soup" setting. Cook for 20 minutes. Once the soup is done, wait for the pressure to subside.
3. Carefully open the pot, remove the thighs with a slotted spoon and allow them to cool.
4. Remove the meat from the bones discarding the bones, skin, and cartilage. Return the meat to the pot with the other ingredients.
5. Taste and adjust the seasoning. Serve hot.

Serving suggestion: Serve hot with ground black pepper.
Tip: You can use other parts of the chicken for this soup.

Cabbage Soup

Serves: 4
Cook time: 25 minutes

Ingredients:

- 1 small green cabbage, roughly chopped
- 750 ml vegetable broth
- 450 gr can diced tomatoes
- 3 carrots, chopped
- 3 stalks celery, chopped
- 1 onion, chopped
- 2 cloves garlic
- 2 tablespoons apple cider vinegar
- 1 tablespoon lemon juice
- 2 teaspoons dried sage
- Salt and pepper to taste
- 3 tablespoons olive oil

Directions:

1) Combine cabbage, vegetable broth, diced tomatoes, carrots, celery, onion, garlic, apple cider vinegar, lemon juice, and sage and put into your Instant Pot. Close and lock the lid. Select High pressure and set at 15 minutes.
2) Release pressure using the natural-release method, which takes about 10 minutes. Unlock and remove lid.
3) Add seasoning and olive oil and cook for another 10 minutes.

Serving suggestion: Serve as a soup or a light meal.

Tip: Can be stored in the fridge for up to five days.

Chicken Stew

Serves: 4
Cook time: 8 hours (on Low)

Ingredients

- 1 kg chicken breast
- 1 onion, chopped
- 1 green bell pepper, chopped
- 1 red chili
- 5 green chilies
- 2 tablespoons coconut oil
- 450 gr can of diced tomatoes
- 200 gr tomato sauce
- 3 garlic cloves, minced
- 1 tablespoon cumin
- 1 tablespoon chili powder
- 2 teaspoons dried oregano
- Salt and pepper, to taste
- Cilantro, to garnish
- Avocado, to garnish

Directions:

1) Put chicken pieces, followed by the rest of the ingredients, into the Instant Po.
2) Set on Low for 8 hours.
3) Once it's cooked, remove the chicken from the Instant Pot and shred it. Return to the Pot, taste and adjust the seasoning.

Serving suggestion: Serve with chopped cilantro or sliced avocado.

Tip: The same soup can be made in much less time, on High pressure, but will not taste the same.

Lamb Stew

Serves: 4-5
Cook time: 35 minutes
Ingredients:

- 1 kg s lamb stew meat, cut into cubes
- 1 acorn squash, peeled, seeded and cubed
- 3 large carrots, sliced
- 1 large onion, sliced
- 1 sprig rosemary (2 if it's small)
- 1 bay leaf
- 6 cloves garlic, thinly sliced
- 3 tablespoons broth, or water
- Salt to taste

Directions:

1. Place all the ingredients into your Instant Pot. Use the Soup/Stew setting and cook for 35 minutes.
2. Carefully release the pressure before unlocking the lid.

Serving suggestion: Serve with roasted potatoes.

Tip: You can use beef or goat meat for this recipe.

Spicy Beef Stew

Serves: 2
Cook time: 40 minutes
Ingredients:

- 2 tablespoons ghee or avocado oil
- 500 gr beef stew meat, cut into cubes
- 1 onion, diced
- 3 medium potatoes, chopped
- 4 carrots, chopped
- 2 celery stalks, chopped
- 2 cups kale leaves, stems removed
- 1 tsp garlic powder
- 1/2 tsp black pepper
- 2 cups bone broth
- 2 tablespoons your favorite hot sauce
- Salt to taste

Directions:

1. Set your Instant Pot to Sauté setting and heat the avocado oil.
2. Add the meat and stir until the meat is browned.
3. Add and stir in the rest of the ingredient, except salt.
4. Close the lid, and make sure the pressure valve is set to "sealing."
5. Set the Instant Pot to Meat/Stew.
6. It will take about 40 minutes to cook. Press the "Cancel" then release the pressure valve. Alternatively, you can wait for the Instant Pot to automatically switch to the "Warm" setting, and keep the food warm for the next 10 hours. In the meantime, the pressure will slowly drop.
7. Taste and adjust seasoning.

Serving suggestion: Serve with mashed potato.
Tip: You can leave out kale, or substitute it with some other vegetables.

Juicy Veal Stew

Serves: 2
Cook time: 6 hours

Ingredients:

- 500 gr veal stew meat, cut into cubes
- 1 tablespoon ghee or coconut oil
- 1 small onion, sliced
- 1 large sweet potato, cubed
- 2 carrots, chopped
- 3 garlic cloves, minced
- Juice of 1 lemon
- 1/4 cup water
- Salt and pepper, to taste
- 2 sprigs of fresh thyme, or 1 teaspoon of dried thyme

Directions:

1. Set the Instant Pot to Saute, melt the ghee and add the meat.
2. Stir until it brown on all sides, about 5 minutes.
3. Set the Instant Pot on Soup/Sew mode, add the vegetables.
4. When the meat is browned, add it to the vegetables and stir.
5. Season with salt and pepper, and place the thyme sprigs over the mixture
6. Pour the lemon juice and water over everything.
7. Put the lid on the slow cooker and cook on low for 6-8 hours.
8. When finished, take out the thyme sprigs before serving.

Serving suggestion: Serve with mashed potatoes.

Tip: If you have a big Instant Pot, where the food is evenly distributed, you may need only 4 hours to cook this meal. The smaller the pot, the longer will it take for the meat to cook.

Oriental Pork Stew

Serves: 5
Cook Time: 45 minutes

Ingredients
- 500 gr pork stew meat, cubed
- 2 tablespoons olive oil to sear the pork
- pinch of sea salt
- 6-8 boiled chicken eggs
- Cilantro leaves and stems, for garnish
- 1 tablespoon dry coriander seeds
- 1 tablespoon ginger grated
- 1 tablespoon black peppercorns
- 2 tablespoon garlic cloves slice lengthwise

For the stew:
- 2 tablespoons 5 spice powder
- 1 cup tamari
- 2 tbsp cacao powder
- 1 ½ tbsp ginger sliced
- 1 cup chopped cilantro include leaves, stems, and roots (if possible)
- 1 medium yellow onion peeled and quartered
- 1 whole garlic head peeled and sliced (you can put them in a cheesecloth)
- 8 cups tap water for a 5-liter size instant pot
- 1 tbsp coarse sea salt

Directions:

1. Place the spices in a mortar and pestle and pound until they are mixed well (alternatively, blend them in a small food processor). Set aside.

2. Press the "Sauté" button and select a "Normal" temperature.
3. Add 2 tablespoons of olive oil and sauté the meat, about 5 minutes. Season with salt.
4. Set the pork aside.
5. Keep the "Saute" function on for next step.

To stew the pork:

1. Add another tablespoon of olive oil to Instant Pot and saute the crushed spices for about 3 minutes. Turn off Saute function key.
2. Add the pork back to the pot. Add all other ingredients.
3. Carefully Seal/Lock the pressure cooker. Select "Meat/Stew" function key and cook for 35 minutes.
4. In the meantime, boil 6-8 chicken eggs on a stove top. When cool, peel and set aside.
5. When the pork is done, add the eggs and let them soak in broth.

Serving suggestion: Serve with sauerkraut or pickled cucumber.

Tip: It tastes even better the following day.

Mushroom Potato Stew

Serves: 4
Cook time: 33 minutes
Ingredients:
- 2 medium sized onions, chopped
- 3 medium carrots, sliced into sticks
- 3 ribs celery, sliced
- 3 medium portabella mushrooms, quartered
- 6 garlic cloves, finely chopped
- 5 cups water
- 1 kg white potatoes, peeled and cut into chunks
- ⅓ cup tomato paste
- 1 tablespoon dried Italian herb seasoning
- 1 tablespoon paprika
- 2 teaspoons finely chopped fresh rosemary
- ½ cup fresh parsley, chopped

Directions:

1. Press the "Sauté" function key on your Instant Pot. Heat 1 tablespoon of water the pot. When the water is hot, add the onions, carrots, and celery, and and cook for about 8 minutes, stirring all the time, and adding water if needed.
2. Stir in the mushrooms and garlic, and continue to cook, stirring all the time, for 5 minutes more, adding water as needed.
3. Add the 5 cups of water, potatoes, tomato paste, Italian seasoning, rosemary, and paprika, and set the function key to the "Soup/Stew mode. ring to a boil, uncovered. Seal the lid and cook for 20 minutes.
4. Once the cooking is done, release the pressure and take out 2 cups of the stew out.
5. Put into a blender, and blend just briefly. Stir the mixture back into the pot to thicken the stew. Stir in the parsley.

Serving suggestions: Serve with boiled potatoes.
Tip: You can use a combination of different mushrooms for this stew.

Hungarian Goulash

Serves: 5
Cook time: 20 minutes
Ingredients:
- 500 gr ground beef
- 2 tablespoons olive oil
- 1 small onion, chopped
- 2 medium carrots, chopped
- 2 cloves garlic, minced
- Salt and ground black pepper
- 3 cups low-sodium beef broth
- 450 gr canned tomato sauce
- 500 gr canned tomatoes, chopped
- 1 tablespoon Worcestershire sauce
- ½ teaspoon dried thyme
- ½ teaspoon oregano
- Parsley, for garnish

Directions:

1. Heat 1 tablespoon olive oil with the Saute setting. Add onions and carrots and saute 3 minutes then add garlic and saute 1 minute longer. Set aside.
2. Heat remaining 1 tablespoon olive oil in pot again using the Saute setting, add beef, season with salt and pepper and cook until browned. Drain excess fat.
3. Add the sauteed vegetables, beef broth, tomato sauce, canned tomatoes, Worcestershire, thyme, oregano. Season with salt and pepper to taste. Bring to the boil.
4. Place lid on Instant Pot and make sure the release valve is set to sealing. Hit the "Soup" button and adjust it to 4 minutes.
5. When time is up, use the quick release method.
6. Serve warm, garnished with parsley.

Serving suggestion: Serve with mashed potato.
Tip:Make your own tomato sauce by combining stewed tomatoes and tomato paste. Season to taste.

Cubano Shredded Beef Stew

Serves: 6-8
Cook Time: 50 minutes

Ingredients:
- 1 tablespoon olive oil
- 1 kg beef steak
- Salt and pepper to taste
- 1 medium-sized onion, sliced
- 4-5 cloves garlic, minced
- 250 ml beef broth
- 450 gr canned diced tomatoes
- 2 big peppers, chopped
- ½ teaspoon dried oregano
- 1 teaspoon ground cumin
- 1 bay leaf
- Seasoning
- ½ cup chopped fresh parsley
- 2 tablespoons vinegar
- A dozen chopped green olives

Directions:
1) Season the steak generously on both sides with salt and pepper.
2) Heat the olive oil in the Instant Potmusing the Saute setting. When the oil is hot, add the meat. Brown the meat well on both sides, then set aside.
3) Add the onions and garlic to the pot, and continue to cook over medium saute heat, stirring frequently, until the onions begin to soften. Add the broth and deglaze and scrape the meat that is stuck to the pot. Add the tomatoes, peppers, and desired seasoning; stir to combine, then add the browned flank steak into the stew.

4) Cover the pressure cooker with the lid, ensuring that the valve is in sealing position. Cook under High pressure for 40 minutes.
5) When the cooking time is up, allow at least 10 minutes for the pressure to release naturally. Open the lid, and shred the meat. Discard the bay leaf, then mix in the parsley, vinegar and green olives. Season to taste.

Serving suggestion: Serve with roasted vegetables.

Tip: Best to make a day ahead.

Creamy Coconut Casserole

Serves: 4
Cook time: 10 minutes
Ingredients:
- 2 tablespoons olive oil
- 1 small onion, quartered
- 1 kg skinless and boneless chicken breast or chicken thighs, cut into cubes
- 2 tablespoons Thai red curry paste
- 1 red bell pepper, chopped
- 750 ml chicken broth
- 2 tablespoons fish sauce or salt to taste
- 1 heaping tablespoon sugar
- 200 ml coconut milk
- 2 1/2 tablespoons lime juice
- Cilantro leaves

Directions:
1) Turn on the Saute mode on your Instant Pot. Add the onion and saute for 10 seconds before adding the chicken.
2) Saute the chicken until the surface turns white. Add the Thai curry paste, bell peppers, and kaffir lime leaves (if using), stir to mix well.
3) Add the chicken broth, fish sauce and sugar. Cover the pot and select High pressure for 10 minutes.
4) When it beeps, turn to Quick Release. When the valve drops, remove the lid carefully, add the coconut milk and lime juice to the soup, stir to mix well.
5) Decorate with cilantro and serve immediately.

Serving suggestion: Serve on a bed of cauliflower "rice".
Tip: For more intense taste, add some hot chilies.

Easy Bone Broth

Serves: 4
Cook time: 2 hours

Ingredients

- 1 chicken carcass (bones)
- 2 carrots, cut in chunks
- 1 cup chopped celery
- 1 tablespoon apple cider vinegar
- 2 teaspoons ground turmeric
- 3 cloves garlic
- 1 teaspoon minced fresh ginger root
- 4 cups warm water, or as needed

Directions

1. Add the chicken bones, and other ingredients into the Instant Pot and add enough water to cover. Close and lock the lid. Select Manual function and set timer for 120 minutes. Allow 10 to 15 minutes for pressure to build.
2. Release pressure using the natural-release method according to manufacturer's instructions. Unlock and remove lid.
3. Let cool slightly and strain using a fine metal strainer to remove all the bits of bones and vegetables. Discard, and serve only the soup.

Serving suggestion: Serve hot, or refrigirate.
Tip: Can be used as a soup, or as stock for other dishes.

Quick Vegetable Broth

Serves: 4
Cook time: 15
Ingredients

- 1 large onion, quartered
- 2 carrots, halved
- 4-5 stalks of celery, halved
- 5-6 cloves of garlic, whole
- 3 inch ginger, peeled
- 4 large mushrooms, sliced
- 700 gr assorted vegetables
- 3 bay leaves
- 10 cups water
- ¼ tsp turmeric
- ¼ tsp garam masala
- 1 tsp black pepper

Directions:
1) Put all ingredients in the Instant Pot and push the Manual button to 15 minutes. Seal the lid and make sure the pressure valve is closed.
2) Once cooked, allow the Instant Pot to depressurize naturally (do not use quick release).

Serving suggestion: Serve hot, or keep in the fridge and use as stock for other dishes.
Tip: Can be made up to four days in advance.

Mushroom Broth

Serves: 6
Cook time: 10 minutes
Ingredients:

- 8 cups water

- 20 gr dried porcini mushrooms
- 6 medium cloves of garlic, peeled and smashed
- scant 1 teaspoon fine grain sea salt
- 1/2 teaspoon freshly ground pepper, or to taste
- a sprig or two of fresh thyme

Directions:
1) Combine all the ingredients in your Instant Pot. Close and make sure it's sealed.
2) Pressure cook on high for 10 minutes. Push quick release button, gently shake the pot, and carefully open it. Season with the salt, pepper, and thyme. Wait a minute or two, stir, and taste. Adjust seasoning.
3) Can be refrigiraed for up to five days.

Serving suggestion: *Use as a soup, or stock for other dishes.*

Tip: *It can last several days in the fridge.*

Vegan Stew

Serves: 2
Cook time: 28 minutes
Ingredients:
- 2 small onions, chopped
- 2 large celery stalks, chopped
- 10 white mushrooms, quartered
- 3 garlic cloves, minced
- 1 litre vegetarian broth
- 5 small potatoes, peeled & cubed
- 5 small carrots, sliced 3/4 inch thick
- 1 teaspoon dried oregano
- 1/2 teaspoon dried thyme
- 1/2 teaspoon ground dry mustard
- 1/4 teaspoon ground bay leaves
- 1/2 teaspoon each salt & pepper
- 2 tablespoons of olive oil

Directions:

1) Press the "Sauté" function key on your Instant Pot. Heat the oil and add the onions, celery, mushrooms, carrots and potatoes and saute, stirring frequently, for about 8 minutes.
2) Add the seasoning and vegetarian broth.
3) Set the function key to the Soup/Stew mode. Seal the lid and cook for 20 minutes.
4) Once the pressure has subsided, open the lid carefully and serve.

Serving suggestion: Serve with boiled potatoes.
Tip: You can use whatever seasonal vegetables are available to make this stew.

Lamb and Potato Stew

Serves 4
Cook time: 1 hour
Ingredients:
- 2 small onions, chopped
- 750 gr lamb stew meat, cut into small pieces
- 2 large celery stalks, chopped
- 10 white mushrooms, quartered
- 3 garlic cloves, minced
- 4 cups vegetable broth
- 5 small potatoes, peeled & cubed
- 5 small carrots, sliced
- 1 teaspoon dried oregano
- 1/2 teaspoon dried thyme
- 1/2 teaspoon ground dry mustard
- 1 small bay leaf
- 1/2 teaspoon each salt & pepper

Directions:

1) Combine the spices - salt, pepper, cumin and coriander – and rub into the lamb. Refrigirate to allow the meat to absorb the flavors for at least 30 minutes.
2) Press the "sauté" button on the Instant Pot. Add coconut oil and when it's hot, add lamb and brown it on all sides (this will have to be done in two batches), then remove from the Instant Pot and set aside.
3) Lower the sauté heat and add onion (add more coconut oil if needed). Sauté for 3 to 5 minutes until onion is translucent. Add garlic, ginger and tomato paste. Sauté about 1 minute, mixing constantly.
4) Add bone broth and cinnamon stick. Add meat back to the pot. Seal the pot and set to cook at High pressure for 25 minutes.

5) Let the pressure release/vent naturally. Open the lid and add the sweet potatoes (and saffron, if using).
6) Cook under high pressure for 10 minutes. When done, press the quick release the valve.
7) Garnish with cilantro or parsley.

Serving suggestion: Serve with mashed potatoes.

Tip: You may double the quantity of mushroom.

Meat Recipes

Beef Curry

Serves: 6
Cook time: 25 minutes

Ingredients:

- 3 tablespoons olive oil, for searing
- 1 kg beef stew meat, cut into small pieces
- Salt and pepper to taste
- 1 big onion, chopped
- 5 teaspoons garlic, minced
- 1 tablespoon ginger, chopped finely
- 1 chili pepper, seeded and chopped finely
- 1 teaspoon freshly ground black pepper
- 1 teaspoon turmeric powder
- 2 cups beef broth
- 2 large carrots, peeled, cut into small pieces
- 2 big potatoes, cut into small pieces
- Salt to taste
- 450 ml can coconut milk, unsweetened
- 1/2 cup cilantro, chopped

Directions:

1. Press the 'Saute' button on Instant Pot. Heat the oil, and working in batches, sear seasoned beef until browned on all sides. Set aside.
2. Turn Instant Pot off and add onions, garlic, ginger, jalapenos and stir well.

3. Press 'Saute' again and add 2 tablespoon broth to deglaze Instant Pot, scraping up all the brown bits.
4. Saute onion mixture till golden brown, about 5 minutes. If the mixture sticks to the bottom, add a tablespoon or two of broth.
5. Add reserved beef, black pepper, turmeric, steak sauce and saute briefly to coat the beef with spices.
6. Add broth and stir. Close Instant Pot Lid, and make sure steam release handle is in the 'Sealing' position.
7. Cook on 'Manual' (or 'Pressure Cook') for 15 minutes (Make sure steam release handle is in the 'Sealing' position). Do a Quick Release.
8. Add potatoes and carrots to Instant Pot. Cook on 'Manual' (or 'Pressure Cook') for 5 minutes.
9. Allow Instant Pot to release naturally for 10 minutes, and release any remaining pressure to open the Instant Pot.
10. Add coconut milk to the Instant Pot beef curry and stir to combine. Taste and season with salt to taste. Press 'Saute' and heat through.

Serving suggestion: To serve, sprinkle with chopped cilantro and serve with boiled potatoes. **Tip:** For more intense flavour, you can add ketchup, Worcestershire sauce, or Dijon mustard.

Sunday Pot Roast

Serves: 4
Cook time: 1 hour 15 minutes
Ingredients:
- 1.5 kg beef roast
- salt to taste
- 4 tablespoons olive oil
- 500 ml beef broth
- 1 pkg onion soup mix
- 1 onion, quartered
- 500gr baby potatoes
- 3 baby carrots, sliced

Directions:

1) Sprinkle pot roast with salt and set aside.
2) Heat 2 tablespoons of olive oil in Instant Pot and set to "Saute".
3) Add pot roast and sear for 4-5 minutes on each side.
4) Add beef broth to Instant Pot.
5) Add vegetables, 2 tablespoons olive oil, and onion soup mix. Stir.
7) Place lid on Instant pot with steam valve closed.
8) Switch Instant Pot setting to "manual" and set for 70 minutes on High pressure
9) Do a natural release for at least 10 minutes, then quick release.
10) Remove roast from instant pot, slice, and serve with vegetables.

Serving suggestion: Serve with a salad and roasted potatoes on the side.
Tip: Add chilies for more flavour.

Leg of Lamb

Serves: 4
Cook time: 35 minutes
Ingredients:

- 1 boneless leg of lamb (about 2 kg)
- Salt and pepper
- 2 tablespoons olive oil
- 500 ml water
- 4 cloves garlic, crushed
- 2 tablespoons chopped fresh rosemary

Directions:

1. Rinse the lamb under running water and pat the dry with paper towels. Season with salt and pepper.
2. Set the Instant Pot to sauté and add the oil. Once the oil is hot, brown the lamb. Remove the lamb and sprinkle garlic and rosemary over the top and sides.
3. Insert the rack into the bottom of the Instant Pot. Pour in the water into the bottom of the pot. Place the lamb on the rack and set the Instant Pot to meat/stew. Cook 30 to 35 minutes. Let the pressure release naturally before removing the lid.
4. Preheat the broiler. Set the lamb on a broiling pan and broil 6 inches from the heat for about 2 minutes, to brown the top. Remove and let rest at least for 10 minutes before slicing.

Serving suggestion: Serve with roasted potatoes.
Tip: Can be made in advance.

Lamb Curry

Serves: 6
Cook time: 25 minutes
Ingredients:

- 750 gr lamb stew meat
- 4 cloves garlic, minced
- 1-inch piece fresh ginger, grated
- 125 ml coconut milk
- Juice of ½ lime
- Salt and pepper to taste
- 1 tablespoon ghee
- 450 gr can chopped tomatoes
- 1 ½ Tbsp. garam masala
- ¾ tsp. turmeric
- 1 medium onion, diced
- 3 medium carrots, sliced
- 1 medium zucchini, diced
- Cilantro, chopped

Directions:

1. Combine meat, minced garlic, grated ginger, coconut milk, lime juice, sea salt and black pepper in a container with a lid. Mix together and marinate in refrigerator for 30 minutes and up to 8 hours.
2. After marinating, combine the meat with marinade, tomatoes, ghee, garam masala, onions and carrots. Lock lid into place then set the steam release handle to 'Sealing'. Select Manual and cook at high pressure for 20 minutes.
3. When the meat is cooked, allow Instant Pot to naturally release pressure for 15 minutes then flip the steam release

handle to 'Venting' to release the remaining steam before attempting to open the lid.
4. Remove the lid then switch the Instant Pot to saute (normal) setting, stir in diced zucchini and simmer for 5-6 minutes without the lid or until zucchini is tender and sauce is slightly thickened.
5. Garnish with chopped cilantro.

Serving suggestion: Serve with roasted potatoes.

Tip: Instead of garam masala you can use yellow curry powder, in which case there is no need for turmeric powder.

Mediterranean Lamb Roast with Potatoes

Serves: 6
Cook time: 1 hour
Ingredients:

- 2 tablespoons olive oil
- 3 kg leg of lamb, bone-in or boneless
- Salt and pepper to taste
- 1 bay leaf, crushed
- 1 teaspoon marjoram thyme and sage, each
- 3 cloves garlic, minced
- 1 teaspoon ginger
- 2 cups broth
- 2-1/2 to 3 pound potatoes, peeled and cut into 2" to 3" pieces
- 2 to 3 tablespoons arrowroot powder + 1/3 cup water (optional)

Directions:

1. Turn Instant Pot to Sauté. Wait until it gets hot, then add olive oil.
2. Put the roast in, and swirl it around so it gets coated with oil.
3. Try to prevent it from sticking to the bottom of the pot.
4. Sear the meat on one side, then flip it over to sear on the other side.
5. Sprinkle the roast with the salt, pepper, and all herbs.
6. Add broth. Lock the lid.
7. If using an electric cooker, set to High pressure for 50 minutes.
8. Once meat is cooked, do a quick pressure release.
9. Open the lid carefully.
10. Add potatoes. Cover the pot and set to High pressure for 10 minutes.

11. When potatoes are cooked, do a quick pressure release. Open the lid.
12. Transfer the potatoes and roast to a serving dish.
13. Cover to keep warm while you make the gravy out of the broth.

Serving suggestion: Serve with roasted potatoes.
Tip: You can have it warm or cold, it's equally delicious.

Pork Chops

Serves: 4
Cook time: 25 minutes

Ingredients:

- 1 kg pork chops, boneless
- Salt and pepper to taste
- 2 tablespoons honey
- 2 tablespoons Dijon mustard
- ½ tablespoon maple syrup
- ½ teaspoons ginger, peeled and minced
- Pinch of cinnamon
- Pinch of cloves

Directions:
- Sprinkle pork chops with salt and pepper and place in the inner pot. Set Instant Pot to Saute.
- Brown pork chops on each side.
- In a bowl, combine honey, Dijon mustard, maple syrup, ginger, cinnamon, cloves and water. Pour over pork chops.
- Lock cover into place and seal steam nozzle.
- Set on the manual setting for 15 minutes.
- Naturally release pressure for 5 minutes and quick release remaining pressure.
- Change setting to Saute to thicken sauce for a few minutes.

Serving suggestion: Serve with horsradish.
Tip: Leave out honey and maple syrup if you prefer more traditional taste.

Holiday Roast

Serves: 4

Cook time 4 hours

Ingredients:

- Pork shoulder
- 1 tablespoon olive oil
- 1 tablespoon coconut oil
- 2 tablespoon Worcester sauce
- 1 tablespoon mixed herbs
- 1 tablespoon rosemary
- 1 chicken stock cube
- Salt and pepper to taste

Directions:

1. Place the olive oil and the coconut oil in the bottom of the Instant Pot. Add the pork shoulder.
2. Scorch the top of the pork. Mix all of the seasonings and the chicken stock cube in a bowl and then rub into the top of your pork.
3. Place the lid on your Instant Pot and cook on the slow cooker setting for 4 hours.
4. Take the lid off and allow to rest for at least 10 minutes before serving.

Serving suggestion: Serve with roasted potatoes.

Tip: If you slash small lines in the meat, spices will drip into the holes as it cookes.

Pork Roast in Mustard Sauce

Serves: 6
Cook tune: 35 minutes
Ingredients:

- 1 kg pork loin roast
- Salt and pepper to taste
- 2 tablespoons butter
- 1/2 medium onion, diced
- 4 cloves garlic, minced
- 2 medium carrots, chopped
- 2 stalks celery, chopped
- 1/2 cup broth
- 2 tablespoons Worcestershire sauce
- 1 tablespoon brown sugar
- 1 teaspoon yellow mustard
- 2 teaspoons herbs of choice (rosemary, basil, oregano, thyme, etc)
- 1 tablespoon corn starch
- 1/4 cup water

Directions:

1. Season pork with salt and pepper. Turn Instant Pot on "Sauté", and melt the ghee. Add the pork loin and sear both sides to a nice golden brown. Add the onions and garlic and cook until soft, about 2 minutes.
2. Stir in the carrots, celery, broth or apple juice, Worcestershire sauce, brown sugar, mustard, and herbs.
3. Close the lid, set to High pressure, and after the pressure cooker reaches full pressure, cook for 15-30 minutes.
4. After the cooking time is complete, press "Cancel" and carefully release the pressure. If possible, check the internal temperature of the pork loin.

5. Remove the meat from the Instant Pot, cover and allow to rest for about 10 minutes, depending on how large your loin roast is and how well done you like it.
6. Mix together the cornstarch and water. Add to the Instant Pot with the juices. Turn Instant Pot on "Sauté" and simmer until thickened. Taste seasoning and add additional salt and pepper if desired.

Serving suggestion: Serve with Coleslaw salad.
Tip: You may use apple juice instead of broth.

Veal Roast

Serves: 2
Cook time: 25 minutes
Ingredients:
- 2 tablespoons olive oil
- 500g veal roast
- 1 onion, roughly sliced
- 1 carrot, roughly sliced
- 1 celery stalk, roughly sliced
- 2 garlic cloves, whole
- 5 bay leaves
- 1 rosemary sprig
- 4 cloves (the spice)
- Salt and pepper to taste
- 2 cups water

Directions:

1. Heat the oil in the Instant Pot. Add the meat and brown on all sides.
2. Move the meat to a dish, and to the empty pressure cooker add the onion, carrot and celery and swooshing them infrequently so they begin to take on a little color.
3. Add the garlic, bay, rosemary and cloves,
4. Put the meat back in the pressure cooker and cover with the salt, pepper, and water.
5. Close and lock the lid of the pressure cooker. Turn the heat up to high and when the cooker reaches pressure, lower to the heat to the minimum required by the cooker to maintain pressure. Cook for 15-25 minutes (depending on the thickness of the roast) at high pressure.
6. When time is up, open the pressure cooker with the Natural release method - move the cooker off the burner and wait for the pressure to come down on its own (about

10 minutes). Then, release the rest of the pressure using the valve.
7. Remove the roast and place on a serving dish to cool.
8. When the roast is relatively cool, wrap tightly and put in the refrigerator to chill.
9. To serve, slice the roast thinly, cover with sauce and sprinkle capers on top.
10. Both the roast and the sauce can be prepared up to a day in advance

Serving suggestion: Slice the roast thinly and serve cold, with a sauce of your choce

Tip: It tastes best if it's made a day ahead.

Veal in Vegetable and Tomato Sauce

Serves: 6
Cook time: 25 min
Ingredients:

- 2 sprigs fresh rosemary, one finely chopped and one for garnish
- 1 tablespoon olive oil
- 1 tablespoon ghee
- 250gr shallots (about 15 small)
- 2 carrots, chopped
- 2 celery stalks, chopped
- 2 tablespoons flour
- 1.5k veal, cut into 1" cubes
- 250 ml tomato, chopped
- water to cover - may be substituted with white veal stock
- 2 teaspoons salt - withhold if using salted stock

Directions:

1. Heat the ghee and oil in the Instant Pot, and add finely chopped rosemary.
2. Add the shallots, carrots and celery and saute until the shallots are just starting to soften.
3. In the meantime, coat the meat cubes in flour.
4. Put the vegetables aside and brown the meat cubes on all sides.
5. Pour in the water and use a spatula or wooden spoon to lift and incorporate any brown bits on the bottom of the cooker.
6. Pour in just enough water (or stock) to almost cover, but not submerge, the meat.
7. Close and lock the lid of the pressure cooker. Turn the heat up to high and when the cooker reaches pressure, lower to the heat to the minimum required by the cooker to

maintain pressure. Cook for 15 to 20 minutes at High pressure.
8. When it's cooked, open the cooker by slowly releasing the pressure.
9. Let the cooker simmer uncovered at medium high heat for about 5 more minutes or until the cooking liquid has thickened to taste.

Serving suggestion: Serve with mashed potato.
Tip: Many people find rosemary too aromatic, so you may want to use less, but don't leave it out completely.

Side Dishes Recipes

Steamed Broccoli

Serves: 2
Cook time: 2 minutes

Ingredients:

- 1 medium broccoli,, cut into florets
- Salt & pepper
- 160 ml water

Directions:

1. Place 160ml of water into the Instant Pot, and place the broccoli on the steamer rack.
2. Place the lid on your Instant Pot and set the valve to sealing. Press Steam for 2 minutes.
3. When it's done, wait for couple of minutes until pressure had dropped.
4. Serve warm or cold, seasoned with salt and pepper.

Serving suggestions: Drizzle with olive oil for creamier taste.
Tip: You can turn steamed broccoli into a salad by adding chopped garlic and black olives, and a salad dressing of your choice.

Garlic Butter New Potatoes

Serves: 2
Cook time: 4 minutes

Ingredients:

- 500 g new potatoes
- 3 tablespoon melted ghee
- 3 cloves garlic, finely chopped
- Handful of rosemary
- Salt & pepper
- 160 ml water

Directions:

1. Add 160ml of water to your Instant Pot.
2. Place your new potatoes into your steamer dish together with the ghee, garlic, fresh herbs and salt and pepper.
3. Place the lid on your Instant Pot and set the valve to sealing. Press steam for 4 minutes.
4. When they are done, leave the potatoes on "keep warm" function for 5 minutes, before opening the lid. Serve warm with extra fresh herbs.

Serving suggestions: Rosemary is a very spicy herb and should be used sparingly. For a slightly milder taste you can use parsley or chives instead of rosemary.

Tip: This recipe can also be used for old potatoes, provided they are chopped into smaller pieces.

Beets Side Dish

Serves: 4
Cook time: 28 minutes
Ingredients:

- 6 medium beets (about 800 gr), cleaned and trimmed
- 250ml cold water

Directions:

1) Pour 250ml cold water in the pressure cooker. Place a steamer basket in the Instant Pot, then place the beets in the basket.
2) Close the lid and cook at High pressure for 28 minutes
3) Immediately release the pressure by turning the venting knob to venting position. Carefully open the lid.
4) Let the beets cool, before peeling them. Cut into quarters and season with salt.
5) Serve cold.

Serving suggestion: You can turn this into a salad if you slice the cooked beets thinly, and drizzle them with olive oil. You can sprinkle them with grated horseradish or cumin seeds.

Tips: Beet stains are sometimes difficult to remove, so you may wear disposable gloves when peeling them. If your clothes becomes stained, soak them in cold water immediately.

Mashed Potatoes

Serves: 2-4
Cook time: 8 minutes
Ingredients:
- 4 big Yukon gold potatoes (about 1100 gr), peeled and quartered
- 250 ml water
- 5 tablespoons melted ghee
- 1 egg yolk
- 2 cloves garlic, minced or finely chopped
- Salt and pepper to taste

Directions:
1) Add 250 ml water into the Instant Pot. Place the vegetable steamer in the pot and place the quartered potatoes in the steamer.
2) Close the lid. Cook in High pressure for 8 minutes, then press quick release.
3) While the potatoes are cooking, melt the ghee and add the garlic. Add a pinch of salt. Sauté the garlic for 1 to 2 minutes until fragrant and golden in color.
4) Remove the lid. Transfer the cooked potatoes into mixing bowl and mash them with a potato masher. Add the garlic ghee mixture to the potatoes. Continue to mash and stir until smooth. Taste and season with salt and pepper.
5) Serve immediately.

Serving suggestions: For creamier taste, you can add 1 egg yolk to the mashed potatoes. You can sprinkle the mashed potatoes with paprika or chopped parsley, prior to serving.

Tips: Even if you decide to double the quantity of potatoes in this recipe, you should only increase the cooking time for 1 minute. Take care not to pack potatoes too tightly in the steamer.

Plain Potatoes

Serves: 4
Cook time: 20 minutes

Ingredients:

- 8 medium sized russet potatoes, of approximately the same size (about 2 kg)
- 2 tablespoons olive oil
- Salt and pepper
- 250 ml water

Directions:
1) Clean the potatoes and poke them with a fork, which will allow the steam to escape and prevent the potatoes from bursting
2) Place 250 ml of cold water and a trivet into the pressure cooker. Place the potatoes on top of the trivet and close the lid. Pressure cook at High pressure for 12 minutes. Adjust your time from 10 minutes (small) to 20 minutes (extra-large) depending on the size of your potatoes. Once the cooking is done, wait for 10 minutes to turn the venting knob to release the pressure. Open the lid carefully.
3) Serve immediately.

Serving suggestion: For even better taste, you can bake the cooked potatoes. Drizzle olive oil over cooked potatoes and place them on a baking tray. Season with salt and pepper and bake in the oven for 10-15 minutes until the skin becomes crisp.

Tip: If you are baking them, drizzle them with olive oil but if you are having them plain, then pour melted ghee over the cooked potatoes, and season to taste with salt, black pepper or paprika.

Boiled Eggs

Serves: 2
Cook time: 5 – 14 minutes, depending on the kind of egg you want

Ingredients:

- 2 large eggs
- 250 ml water

Directions:

1. Place steam rack inside the pressure cooker and add 250 ml of cold water to the pot. Place the eggs at the center of the rack.
2. Close lid. Pressure cook at **Low Pressure - for** soft boiled egg for 5, for hard boiled egg, for 14 minutes. For large eggs, we recommend reducing the pressure cooking time by 1 minute.
3. Once time is up, immediately quick release, ie press the cancel button on your Instant Pot right away).
4. Open lid. Immediately place the eggs in a bowl of cold water for couple of minutes. Change the water couple of time, until the eggs have cooled down.

Serving suggestion: To make a sandwich spread, you can add mashed cooked egg yolks to sardines, and softened butter. Season to taste.
Tip: Never boil eggs for less than 3 minutes.

Sweet Potatoes

Serves: 4
Cook time: 15-50 minutes, depending on the size

Ingredients:

- 2 – 4 whole sweet potatoes (about 700 gr)
- 250 ml cold water

Directions:
1) Scrub the sweet potatoes in cold water
2) Add 250 ml of cold water and a steamer rack in the Instant Pot.
3) Place whole sweet potatoes on the steamer rack, and close the lid.
4) Pressure cook the sweet potatoes for 15 minutes (if small) to 50 minutes (if very big).
5) Serve immediately.

Serving suggestion: You can drizzle them with butter, or maple syrup.

Tip: No need to peel sweet potatoes, provided you rinse and scrub them well prior to cooking.

Butter Squash

Serves: 4

Cook time: 6-12 minutes, depending on whether you are cooking it whole, or cubed

Ingredients:

- About 1 kg of butter squash cut in half and cleaned, or peeled and cubed
- 250 ml water

Directions:

1) Place your trivet or steamer basket into your Instant Pot. Add water and squash. Close lid and set valve to Sealing.
2) Set your Instant Pot to manual mode, and cook the squash at High pressure for 6 -12 minutes, depending on whether it's whole or cubed.
3) Once the manual cooking program finishes, wait 5 minutes before you perform a quick release of the pressure. This adds up to about 25 minutes time spent in the Instant Pot as it can take up to 10 minutes for the pot to reach pressure.
4) Carefully remove your squash halves (or cubes) to a large mixing bowl, and remove flesh carefully with a spoon.

Serving suggestion: Serve with the main meal seasoned with melted ghee, salt and pepper, or as a very healthy dessert sprinkled with cinnamon (instead of sugar you can add chopped dried figs or dates).

Tip: Chopped squash cooks quickly, but peeling and chopping takes time. You may decide to buy pre-cut butternut squash cubes. Depending on the size of the cubes, and your own taste, you may decide to increase, or decrease cooking time.

Cauliflower Mash

Serves: 2
Cook time: 5 minutes

Ingredients:

- 1 large head of cauliflower, cored and cut into large florets
- 250 ml of water
- 2 tablespoons melted ghee
- salt, pepper, garlic powder, chopped chives, green onions,

Directions:

1. Place the steamer basket inside the Instant Pot, add water, and place the cauliflower on the steamer basket. Close the lid, set valve to sealing.
2. Cook on Manual High pressure for 5 minutes.
3. Immediately quick release the pressure and open the lid.
4. Carefully remove the inner pot to drain the water.
5. Return cauliflower to a cleaned and empty inner pot.
6. Add butter and seasonings. Mash until smooth.
7. Serve hot or cold.

Serving suggestion: Drizzle with melted ghee and sprinkle with chopped chives, green onions, etc.

Tip: If you are trying to reduce your calorie intake, you can eliminate ghee from the recipe.

Steamed Vegetables

Serves:
Cook time: 8 minutes

Ingredients:

- 4 medium-sized carrots, chopped
- 4 medium-sized potatoes, chopped
- 1 big leeks, chopped
- 100 gr of dried mushrooms, previously soaked in warm water for 20 minutes
- 200 gr Brussels sprouts (or cauliflower, or cabbage)
- 100 ml water
- Salt and pepper to taste

Directions:

1) Clean and rinse the vegetables.
2) Place the steamer basket inside the Instant Pot, add 100 ml water, and place the vegetables on the steamer basket.
3) Close the lid, set valve to sealing and press Steam for 8 minutes.
4) When it's done, wait for couple of minutes until the pressure had dropped.
5) Serve warm.

Serving suggestion: You can drizzle with soy sauce, ketchup, or olive oil, or simply sprinkle with paprika, salt and pepper.

Tip: You can use almost any vegetable for this dish, but to get the best results, choose vegetables which require approximately the same cooking time, eg broccoli can be cooked in 2 minutes, while potatoes will require much longer.

Good Luck!

Thanks for reading this book! Dear readers!

Hope you will got your best choice by reading this cookbook!

Wish you will have a good and healthy life!

Best wishes to you and your family!

Printed in Great Britain
by Amazon